faith

IN THE FACE OF

empire

faith
IN THE FACE OF
empire

The Bible Through Palestinian Eyes

MITRI RAHEB

ORBIS BOOKS

Maryknoll, New York 10545

Third Printing, October 2014

Published by Orbis Books, Box 302, Maryknoll, NY 10545–0302.

Manufactured in the United States of America.

Manuscript editing and typesetting by Joan Weber Laflamme.

Library of Congress Cataloging-in-Publication Data

Raheb, Mitri.
Faith in the face of empire : the Bible through Palestinian eyes / Mitri Raheb.
    pages cm
   Includes bibliographical references.
   ISBN 978-1-62698-065-5 (pbk.)
    1. Christianity and politics. 2. Imperialism. I. Title.
BR115.P7R2315 2014
261.7089'9274--dc23

        2013031307

In memory of my father, Bishara Mitri Raheb,
who instilled in me faith and embodied creative resistance.

Contents

Acknowledgments

This book was written during a stay at Yale Divinity School in the summer of 2012. I would like to acknowledge with gratitude the support of many friends and colleagues whose efforts have made the publishing of this book possible: John Lindner, the director of the Department of External Relations at Yale Divinity School, for his friendship and for making this stay possible and enjoyable; the librarians at Yale Divinity School under the leadership of Paul Stuehrenberg, who were always helpful and supportive; and the Overseas Mission Study Center (OMSC) for its hospitality. A special thanks goes to Ms. Sara Makari, who worked on editing the manuscript, and to Robert Ellsberg from Orbis Books for reviewing the manuscript and offering many valuable suggestions. I'm thankful to all those at Orbis for their interest in bringing this book into the American market.

Introduction

Jesus was a Middle Eastern Palestinian Jew. If he were to travel through Western countries today, he would be "randomly" pulled aside and his person and papers would be checked. The Bible is a Middle Eastern book. It is a product of that region with all of its complexities. While it might seem that I am stating the obvious, I firmly believe that this notion has not been given enough attention. In fact and in spite of being a Middle Easterner, I have come to discover the importance of the geo-politics of the region only in the last ten years. I began to sense that it was not merely by chance that the three monotheistic religions and their sacred scriptures, for good or for bad, hailed from the same region. The starting point for this approach, as well as for this book, is geo-politics. For me, as a Palestinian Christian, the realization of this fact made for a fascinating discovery.

This discovery did not come to light in an academic setting somewhere in the West, and it was not the outcome of a study I undertook in a research center. It was, instead, the gradual accumulation of knowledge I gained "in the field" by observing the movements and processes occurring in Palestine over a prolonged period. In short, I was observing, analyzing, and trying to understand what was happening around me. In that sense this book is not "less scientific" for not having been developed in a Western academic setting with Western methodology; I would argue that it is "more scientific" because it is based on lengthy and measured observation on the ground in Palestine. Observation is the mother of science. Observation helps us identify patterns or logical facts even if we feel that things are utterly illogical and unpredictable. I have been observing the geo-political and socio-religious fields in Palestine daily for the last twenty years. But I am also a pastor; I have to walk to the pulpit Sunday after Sunday to "translate" scripture to those sitting in the pews. And as a pastor I refuse to separate the reality of this world from the reality of the Bible by preaching a "cheap gospel" that neither challenges reality nor is challenged by it. This particular challenge, which is personal, ongoing, and deeply serious, is the environment in which I made this discovery.

What I present here is a theology from and for the Palestinian context. But again, this should not undermine the outcome, or question its seriousness. On the contrary, I believe that living the struggle of Palestine, as a Christian who wrestles daily with scripture, and as an academician, who seeks to analyze and understand what is going on around me, has provided me with a unique environment and setting for such a discovery. The parameters for this experiment are living on Palestinian soil, under Israeli occupation, as a Christian. This book is my attempt to document this experience so that the findings will not be lost but will be available for a wider audience to build upon. The setting of this experiment is highly singular; it might not be possible to replicate it in the future. The stark reality of the yearly decreasing percentage of Christians in Israel-Palestine and throughout the Middle East will remove an important component—the Christian element—of the setting for this book. My generation might be the last in Palestine to struggle with scripture and its meaning in its original context of permanent occupation.[1]

When I went to Yale Divinity School in June 2012 to write this book, I thought I knew how it would look. My intention was to introduce a new theory in biblical hermeneutics, one that I have been developing for almost a decade. I wanted it to be an academic work that would speak mainly to theologians and students of theology in a language with which they are familiar. Yet, after a week of discerning, I decided that this is not who I am. Instead of writing a book about methodologies and fundamentals that would be understood only by experts in theology, I opted to write a popular book that would be accessible to laypeople who are looking for the Bible to make sense, but also for those who are interested in the Middle East in general and the Palestinian-Israeli conflict in particular, as well as the millions of others who feel the heat of the empire in their daily struggle. Instead of discussing the theory of hermeneutics, I decided to lay out how the actual reading of the Bible in the Middle East today might, could, and should look. To give the work a theological framework, I inserted two chapters that are academic in nature. The first chapter, therefore, starts with my understanding of history in relationship to the biblical story and to the formation of identity. For me, as a Palestinian Christian, Palestine is the land of both my physical and my spiritual forefathers and foremothers. The biblical story is thus part and parcel of my nation's history, a history of continuous occupation by succeeding empires. In fact, the biblical story can best be understood as a response to the geopolitical history of the region.

People who are acquainted with my previous books will find in this monograph a new language, approach, and perspective that differ from some of my earlier writings. In those efforts, I now realize, I was dancing to the rhythm of European organ music and theology. I wanted to show that I had mastered the tools of European methodologies, and I tried to utilize them to defend my case as a Palestinian Christian. With this book I feel that I am composing notes for the beat of the drums that constitute the main musical instruments in the Middle East. After a long journey in and through Anglo-Saxon theology,

I sense that I have finally landed in the Middle East, where I belong. The work is thus an invitation to the reader to join me on a journey to the heart of the Middle East and into the heart of the biblical message.

The second chapter of the book shows that with this approach I'm not out of tune with the larger human disciplines but that a highly interesting process has been taking place since the late 1970s that has paved the way for a new reading of history as well as the biblical story. Although such an understanding is not part of the dominant culture, there has already been a great deal written within Palestinian, Israeli, and European circles, as well as from the southern hemisphere, that has enabled such a pathway. This book builds on these recent developments by applying new methodologies to the Palestinian context, thus creating a new and genuine Palestinian theological narrative that takes both the original context of the Bible as well as the current political context seriously.

Chapter 3 opens with a closer look at the geo-politics of the region called the Middle East. The emergence of five regional powers around the first millennia BC and the development of those powers later into formidable empires have shaped the fate of Palestine throughout the last twenty-five hundred years as an occupied territory and a battlefield for competing empires. The occupation of Palestine by Israel today is thus another link in a long chain of uninterrupted occupation. Such occupation is the defining feature of our history, beginning with the Assyrians (722 BC), the Babylonians (587 BC), and the Persians (538 BC), followed by the Greeks (333 BC), the Romans (63 BC), the Byzantines (326), the Arabs (637), the Tartars (1040), the Crusaders (1099), the Ayyubids (1187), the Tartars (1244), the Mamluks (1291), the Mongols (1401), the Ottomans (1516), the British (1917), and the Israelis (1948/67), to name just the major occupiers. This harsh geo-political reality is the content of the fourth chapter.

The fifth chapter depicts what life under the empire has meant for the people of Palestine and what it means for us today. Empires create their own theologies to justify their occupation. They create matrices of control for people and goods. Such oppression generates a number of important questions among the occupied: "Where are you, God?" and "Why doesn't God interfere to rescue his people?" When, under various regimes, diverse identities emerge in different parts of Palestine, the question arises, "Who is my neighbor?" And finally, "How can liberation be achieved?" is a constant question Palestine, giving rise to numerous answers from different religious, political, and social groups. As long as the occupation continues, people will ask, "When are we going to have our own state?" These questions and the differing responses can be found in the Bible, just as they are found in Palestine today. They are discussed in the sixth chapter.

The seventh chapter introduces faith in God as the power that challenges the empire and as an important factor in changing the status quo. God comes into the Middle East to defeat the geo-politics of the region. Reading the Bible with such a lens shows that Jesus understood the geo-politics of the region like no one else. Born under Roman occupation and crushed on the cross by the empire, Jesus was able to draw the vision of a kingdom much bigger than Palestine and more powerful than the empire. He understood his mission to liberate his people by restoring among them a sense of community and by empowering them to become ambassadors of the new kingdom. Jesus' understanding of politics is explained in Chapter 8.

The spirituality required in the Middle East to move forward today is the content of the ninth chapter. Nonviolent and creative resistance, liberty and freedom, equality for women, and a culture of an abundant life are important ingredients for the future of Palestine and the Middle East.

Can we imagine another Middle East? Can there be a different future? These are important questions in the Bible as well as in the context of the current Arab Spring. Prophetic imagination helps us see beyond the current realities, and Christian hope empowers us to move to put a new vision into action.

This book was the outcome of a personal challenge, but I am certain that its outcome will be an even bigger challenge to many others. To Palestinians, it will be challenging because this is not the way they are used to understanding their identity and because the findings do not promise a quick end to the occupation. Second, numerous mainstream Christians, Zionist Jews, and biblical scholars will find this approach challenging because it questions many of their Western assumptions. But, as R. S. Sugirtharajah notes, "This mainstream scholarship is insular and obsessed with its own fixed and rigid Eurocentric questions. . . . On the whole, current biblical scholarship has generated artificial needs and convoluted the biblical histories, complicated textual reconstruction and led its readers astray from the true needs and wants of people."[2]

Seven years ago the Diyar Consortium in Bethlehem launched a ten-year plan of interdisciplinary research on the issue named "Shaping Communities in Times of Crises: Land, Peoples, and Identities."[3] The idea behind the project was to analyze trends in the developments of theological discipline in the last hundred years and to see their implication vis-à-vis the Palestinian issue; at the same time it aimed to develop a new narrative that reclaims its Middle Eastern roots and gives voice to the subaltern people of Palestine so that they can continue telling their story in the face of the empire in the manner of their forefathers and foremothers. This book is but another expression of this project.

Its aim is to lay the groundwork for a genuine Palestinian Christian narrative that is politically relevant and theologically creative. It introduces a new understanding of the biblical narrative and of the mission of Jesus, in which the Palestinian context today serves as a hermeneutical key to understanding the original context and content of the Bible. The Palestinian people are, after all, an important continuum from biblical times to the present. Their narrative sheds a unique light on the biblical narrative. This book is just a start. I hope that others will follow.

I

History and the Biblical Story

HISTORY AS A *LONGUE DURÉE*

Historical writing by Christians that takes account of the Near East and Palestine falls, without exception, into one of two approaches. The first is biblical history, which starts approximately with Abraham and continues, give or take, up to the time of Jesus. Scholars in this field apply their research to the history of the Assyrians, Babylonians, Persians, Greeks, and Romans, and then reflect on the implication of those empires on Palestine. This stream of history generally ends with the second Jewish Revolt in the middle of the second century AD. Because this field is concerned with biblical history, interest in the history of Palestine ends there. After that no one is obliged to hear, study, or even research anything that has to do with the Palestinian history that follows.

The second approach is that of church history. Church history is taught mainly as world history and mainly as Western history. It usually begins with the early church, proceeding from Constantine and the Byzantine Empire to the Holy Roman Empire, the Crusades, the era of Scholasticism, to the Reformation, and on to mission history, concluding with contemporary history. With the exception of the first two centuries and, to a certain degree, the Crusades, Palestine is

9

not deemed noteworthy, and thus its history remains largely in the dark.

This does not make sense to me at all. As a Palestinian, the history of my country can be traced from primeval times until the present. For Palestinians, the Romans were not the last empire. Our history continued after the Romans with the Byzantines (332), Arabs (637), Tartars (1040), Crusaders (1099), Ayyubids (1187), Tartars (1244), Mamluks (1291), Mongols (1401), Ottomans (1516), British (1914), and Israelis (1948/67), to name just the main occupiers.

The same is true for church history, which covers the period from the birth of the church in Jerusalem at Pentecost up to the present. Biblical history happens to a great extent to be the history of my country. As a Palestinian, biblical history is part and parcel of the history of my ancestry. When I read biblical history, I know it is not the history of a country in the "middle of nowhere" or to the "east of something," but it is *our* history. There is, therefore, a smooth connection for me between biblical history and church history. There is no disconnect. This perspective helps me to look at history holistically.

What is true for Christian scholars is true also for secular modern historians. Whether it is in Middle Eastern and North African studies or in political science, one observation can be made. In looking at the myriad works on the Israeli-Palestinian conflict, all start at some point in the late nineteenth century with the beginning of the Zionist movement. Scholars have studied every conceivable aspect of this conflict. And yet all of these studies are done in historic isolation. They lack the historic depth of the centuries and, while they focus on the uniqueness of the current conflict, they fail to see it as part of an ongoing pattern. This historic disconnect leads to false political analyses, for which the Palestinians are paying a high price.

With these two disconnects there are two trends in studying the history of Palestine. Scholars deal either with ancient "sacred historiography," with little political relevance for Palestinians today, or with current "secular historiographies," which stand by themselves with no tie to preceding history. One group espouses biblical history and nothing else, while the other focuses solely on colonial history. Both are studied within separate disciplines with distinct tools and theories. No one wants to mix biblical studies with modern questions arising from the current conflict, and no secular historian is ready to be challenged by what is perceived as a religious discourse.

In this book I look at the history of Palestine, ancient and modern, as a continuous history, with diverse and unique contexts, yet with recurring themes. While I appreciate the telephoto lens that enables us to take a closer look at historic incidences, I want to use the *longue durée*[1] lens to look at history over a longer period and as a continuum. For me, as a historian, the Israeli-Palestinian conflict is an inseparable aspect of European colonial history. It was, after all, the British Empire that planted Israel in the Middle East, and it is the Western world that continues to sustain Israel militarily, financially, and ideologically. This is what I call here empire. Yet, I also see how the entire Bible, both Old and New Testaments, struggles to find a faithful response to various and recurring empires. I understand *sacred* history to be one response to the *secular* histories of brutal empires. As powerful empires continue to be a recurrent theme in the history of Palestine, the question of God remains crucial, and faith is both challenged and engaged.

HISTORY AND IDENTITY

My father was born in 1905 in Bethlehem as an Ottoman citizen with Ottoman identification papers. As a teenager he witnessed the Ottomans being replaced by the British, and suddenly, almost overnight, he became a citizen of Mandate Palestine with a Palestinian passport issued by the British Mandate government. In 1949, when Bethlehem became part of Jordan, he became suddenly a citizen of the Hashemite Kingdom of Jordan. And when he died in 1975, he died under Israeli occupation with an ID card issued by Israel. But he was the same person throughout those geo-political vicissitudes and had no choice but to adjust to changing political and imperial realities.

Throughout Palestinian history empires have occupied the land for a certain number of years but were then forced to leave. Most of the time an empire departed only to make space for another empire. The majority of the native people of the land seldom left. Throughout history and starting with the Assyrian Exile, only a small minority was deported, and only a small percentage decided to leave. The vast majority of the native people remained in the land of their forefathers (2 Kgs 25:11). They remained the *Am Haaretz*, the native "People of the Land," in spite of the diverse empires controlling that land. This is why in this book I choose the people of the land as the description for the native inhabitants throughout history, for it is they who are the enduring continuum.

Their identity, however, was forced to change and develop according to the new realities and empires in which they found themselves. They changed their language from Aramaic to Greek to Arabic, while their identity shifted from Canaanite, to Hittite, to Hivite, to Perizzite, to Girgashite, to Amorite, to Jebusite, to Philistine, Israelite, Judaic/Samaritan, to Hasmonaic, to Jewish, to Byzantine, to Arab, to Ottoman, and to Palestinian, to mention some. The name of the country also changed from Canaan to Philistia, to Israel, to Samaria and Juda, to Palestine. The people changed religion too, from Baal to Jahwe. Later, many believed in Jesus Christ and became Christian. Where the first Aramaic-speaking Christians were "monophysites," they were forced to become Greek Ortho-dox. Forced to pay extra taxes, many joined Islam and became Muslims. And yet they stayed, throughout the centuries, and remained the people of the land with a dynamic identity. In this sense Palestinians today stand in historic continuity with biblical Israel. The native people of the land are the Palestin-ians. The Palestinian people (Muslims, Christians, and Palestin-ian Jews) are a critical and dynamic continuum from Canaan to biblical times, from Greek, Roman, Arab, and Turkish eras up to the present day. They are the native peoples, who survived those empires and occupations, and they are also the remnant of those invading armies and settlers who decided to remain in the land to integrate rather than to return to their original homelands. The Palestinians are the accumulated outcome of this incredible dynamic history and these massive geo-political developments.

This understanding isn't necessarily the dominant one among Palestinians, Europeans, or Israelis. Some Palestinians have adopted a Western lens, seeing themselves as pure Ca-naanites or Arabs who hail from the desert. That the Palestin-ians are no other people than the natives of the land went lost. Interestingly, such an understanding was not unusual among the first Jewish immigrants.[2] Ber Borochov, one of the leaders of the Zionist Left, trying to win the Jews to opt for Palestine during the Uganda controversy, writes:

> The local population in Palestine is racially more closely related to the Jews than to any other people, even among the Semitic ones. It is quite probable that the fellahin in Palestine are direct descendants of the Jewish and Canaanite rural population, with a slight admixture of

Arab blood. . . . Hence, the racial difference between the diaspora Jews and the Palestinian fellahin is no more marked than between Ashkenazi and Sephardic Jews.[3]

In 1918, David Ben-Gurion, the future prime minister of Israel, and Yitzhak Ben-Zvi, the future president, co-wrote a socio-historical book entitled *Eretz Yisrael in the Past and Present.* The book states:

The fellahin are not descendants of the Arab conquerors, who captured Eretz Israel and Syria in the seventh century CE. The Arab victors did not destroy the agricultural population they found in the country. They expelled only the alien Byzantine rulers, and did not touch the local population.[4]

Ben-Gurion and Ben-Zvi came to the conclusion that, "despite the repression and suffering, the rural population remained unchanged." It was this conclusion that, in fact, brought many of the first Jewish immigrants to Palestine, convinced that they would meet in the Palestinians, according to Belkind, "a good number of our people . . . our own flesh and blood."[5]

HISTORY AND MEMORY

History is neither linear nor horizontal; it is not perceived as either a sequence of equal events or a set of facts. As Philip Davies observes:

What is more important about the past than facts? The answer is memory, because memory, whether personal or collective, belongs to us. It is our history. Nor is it a disinterested recollection, but something basic to our identity and our future. Our memory of what we have experienced enables us at each moment to sustain identity. Total amnesia is a total loss of self. We are, except in a purely biological sense, what we remember.[6]

Three developments amongst the Palestinians led to the loss of part of our historical and continuous memory. First, there was an ecclesial amnesia. The historical church that came to prevail in Palestine was the Greek Orthodox Church, which was the outcome and late heir of the Byzantine Empire. Its status as an imperial church made it impossible to recognize the anti-imperial dimension of the Bible. On the contrary, the Bible was de-politicized. For it to make sense to the people of the empire, allegorical and topological methods were used that cut away all geo-political dimensions, except for pilgrimages that supported the imperial economy and allowed it to develop and control the holy sites.

Second, there was a religious amnesia. With the coming of Islam to Palestine in the seventh century, another disconnect to that history was added. With the Islamicization of the people of Palestine the tie to biblical memory was lost and replaced with another that was severed from the geography of Palestine. Neither the Bible nor Palestine was crucial any longer.

The third amnesia was political. The influx of Jewish immigrants into Palestine in the late nineteenth and early twentieth centuries forced the native people of Palestine to erase their biblical memory because it was perceived as a kind of divine legitimization aimed at colonizing their land. With the establishment of a state with a biblical name—Israel—on their homeland, Palestinians had to disconnect from their roots. What was once obvious in terms of historic continuity was gone. The people of Palestine lost their long-term memory. All that remained was their short-term memory, with the *Nakba* of 1948 as their modern history's defining moment.[7]

At the same time there were people of Jewish faith scattered in different countries throughout the world for whom the Old Testament was part of their religious memory yet without a geographical dimension. Their relationship to Palestine was not much different than that of Western Christians. And their relationship to Palestine was mainly as the Holy Land—the land connected to distant historic memory. In fact, historically, Western Christians have had a much greater desire to control the Holy Land and settle in it than their fellow Jews. In the context of nineteenth-century European nationalism, Europeans felt that the Jews did not belong in Europe. They were seen as strangers. The historical memory of Christians located them in a distant country called Palestine. Once the empire took hold of Palestine, it began to facilitate the migration of Jews to Palestine. With little or no connection to the land and its history, Jewish immigrants knew that if they could not belong to Europe, they would prefer to identify with Palestine.

If the decisive moment in modern times for Palestinians was the catastrophe of 1948 and the loss of large parts of historic Palestine, the Holocaust became the decisive moment for modern Jewish history but also a pivotal element for Western Christian memory. From the 1940s on, Europe and the West have chosen to remember the Jews only as victims, the ultimate victims of history. The fact that Israel has developed, in the interim, to become the seventh-largest military power in the world, with nuclear weapons and an advanced military industrial complex, does not take hold of Western consciousness.[8] The impression one sometimes senses hearing the news in the United States is that Palestine is threatening Israel. Defending the security of the State of Israel thus becomes the ultimate "sacred cow" in Israeli as well as in Western politics.

HISTORY AND MYTH

Jan Assmann writes:

> History turns into myth as soon as it is remembered, narrated, and used, that is, woven into the fabric of the present. Seen as an individual and as a social capacity, memory is not simply the storage of past "facts" but the ongoing work of reconstructive imagination. In other words, the past cannot be stored but always has to be "processed" and mediated.[9]

The developments in nineteenth- and twentieth-century Europe led to the "invention of the Jewish People,"[10] who were to replace the people of Palestine. To make that possible, both political power and mythology were necessary as imperial theology became the raison d'être.

Monumental efforts were made by the State of Israel and Jewish organizations globally in branding the new state as a biblical entity. A prime example of this branding was to call the ship that carried Jewish immigrants to Palestine in 1947 *Exodus*. A novel published in 1958 by the well-known Jewish author Leon Uris had the same name as the ship and told the story of those immigrants. The book was made into a Hollywood movie in 1960 and was a huge box-office success. The film *Exodus* was an exemplary piece of Zionist propaganda; it had enormous influence on how Americans began to perceive, or better, misperceive, the Arab-Israeli conflict.[11]

The branding of the state as the biblical Israel accelerated after the War of 1967, when the State of Israel occupied the West Bank, the Gaza Strip, and the Golan Heights. The name chosen for the war—Six Days—also had strong biblical connotations. The victory was identified by many as little "David" (meaning the State of Israel) defeating the giant "Goliath" (meaning the Arab world). Moreover, the conquest of East Jerusalem became the theme of the song "Jerusalem, City of Gold," which was the hit of the year in 1967, perpetuating the image of two thousand years of longing for the eternal city. The song also portrays the myth of Israel as returning to a barren land, to dry fountains, and to the "temple mountain."[12]

The outcome of the 1967 war gave a boost to Jewish religious nationalism and to "messianic" extremist Jewish groups within Israel, who started settling in the West Bank, claiming it as ancient Judea and Samaria. The combination of Judea and Samaria was not so much a geographical description as a religious claim with a political agenda. A process of "Judeaization" of the country soon began, with settlers building Jewish settlements on every tel that had a biblical connection. The occupation of the West Bank, Gaza, and East Jerusalem also greatly benefited Israeli archeologists, who shifted their focus to the West Bank, in general, and to Jerusalem and the Temple, in particular. Consequently, in the course of the last forty years, a gargantuan theft of antiquities has occurred, emptying Palestine of its archeological treasures and destroying many of those seen as "non-Israelite."[13] The appetite of Jewish archeologists after 1967 was such that many of them, like Dayan and Aharoni, advocated a greater Israel after the "Kingdom of David."[14] In this post-1967 discourse, the native Palestinian people were seen as the Canaanites whose land had to be occupied by Israel. The so-called modern-day Canaanites can thus be tolerated only as servants and cheap laborers under an almost "divine Jewish race." Some radical Jewish groups openly called for the ethnic cleansing of the Palestinian people based on biblical passages that propagated the extermination of the Canaanites and other native groups of ancient Palestine.[15]

Israel's military victory in 1967 also had a huge impact on Christians worldwide.[16] The David-and-Goliath myth circulated endlessly among many Christian groups globally, not only in the West. I remember once being told by an Indonesian Christian that his church had prayed earnestly during the 1967 war for Israel to defeat the Arabs. That victory was seen by many as divine intervention. The myth of Israel bringing the "desert to bloom" became widespread in church circles, and a vast number of Christians thought that they were seeing divine history unfold before their eyes. In response, and unsurprisingly, Christian fundamentalism began experiencing a renaissance. Meanwhile, the native peoples of the land (the Palestinians) were silenced politically by the military and economic occupation of their land and became theologically invisible. Indeed, they have been totally replaced by the Israelis, as though they never existed, and as if the land had been kept unpopulated or *terra nullius* (land belonging to no one). This myth was so prevalent and powerful that even some Palestinian scholars bought into it, urging Palestinians to identify with the Canaanites to prove that their Canaanite ancestors preceded the Israelites, as if this would somehow guarantee more entitlement to the land. In short, they were attempting to reconstruct a Palestinian national identity traceable to Canaanite and Jebusite roots. Philip Davies is right in saying that "in Palestine itself a vicious struggle is being fought by people who will not tolerate the difference between a real history and a cultural memory."[17]

HISTORY AND STORY

What such Jewish and Palestinian mythologies have in common is their static understanding of history. That is, they choose one specific moment in ancient history to relate to, as if history has stood still and as if the land was empty. In this book I opt for a dynamic understanding of history as an accumulative process that is ongoing and is open to the future. With a static understanding of history we get stuck. Alternatively, a dynamic understanding of history carries with it endless options for the future. This is why I love these words in the First Epistle of John, "It is not yet made manifest what we shall be" (1 Jn 3:2). Knowing the diverse identities that the people of the land had to undergo tells me that with my current identity I am not at the end. My identity is still in process. And I am not just an object but a subject who has a say in how identity is shaped and how history develops. This was the fascinating message of the prophets: people have a voice in how the story, their story, continues and unfolds. They can make choices.

As Rafiq Khoury writes:

And it is here where we distinguish two types of narratives, two types of memories: the closed ones and the creative ones; memory as prison and memory as prophecy. As a prison, memory could mummify us in a certain time and place and prevent us from getting out of it. According to that meaning, memory is no more a stimulant, but a paralyzing reality. It paralyzes our vitality and creativity. We ruminate on the past, but we remain unable to imagine the future. We are no more able to invent history. As a prophecy, memory is a stimulant. It helps us, on the basis of our vivid memory, to go forward and invent a new future and a new untold narrative.[18]

A static understanding of history always looks backward. Yet for humans, there is no way to return to the past. The only option is to move on. The risen Lord is always "ahead" of us not behind (Mk 16:7).

The Bible is not a book of history but a single, though lengthy, story. It is not interested in revealing "what was then" but "what it meant"—what history meant for the people of Palestine. The people of Palestine were good storytellers, which is why they have kept their story open ended. They want to share it and thereby invite the world to find meaning in the face of the empire. It is with these stories that our forefathers were able to face the empires in which they found themselves for a millennium. These stories generated so much power that they enabled the people of Palestine to survive against almost impossible odds and often to thrive in spite of those empires. When everything had fallen apart and when nothing seemed to have any meaning, our ancestors continued telling their singular story. While empires with their might dictated and wrote history by force, the people of Palestine were writing stories. Indeed, the only product that Palestine has been able to export successfully in its history is those stories. And, ironically, it was those tales emanating from Palestine that often made history.

Because the story is an open-ended one, the key lies in how to tell it and how to interpret it. As Philip Davies notes: "Stories are never innocent of point of view, plot, ideology, or cultural values. We tell our stories of the past in a historical context, looking at the past from a particular point: the present. We cannot be objective, neutral observers. . . . Our views of the past are also affected by our geographical, political, and social location."[19]

This is why interpretation is critical. The one who interprets assumes power; the one who dominates the story makes it his-story, her-story, literally creating history.

2

A Prelude
to a Palestinian Narrative

Hermeneutics is the study of the theory and practice of interpretation. Interpreting a story is an art that requires much creativity and imagination. It is also a science. It is not an innocent science, but one very closely related to empire. The empire wants to control the storyline—its meaning, production, and marketing. It does so consciously and often—far more dangerously—unconsciously.

Hermeneutics is one of the most hazardous and repressive elements in the Israeli-Palestinian conflict. Our problem would be much easier to deal with if it were solely a massive injustice, a problem between Israelis and Palestinians. Unfortunately, the Western world is part of the intractability rather than part of the solution. The Israeli occupation is subsidized by the United States and Europe. The Israelis would not have the financial capability to build a three billion dollar "separation wall" or the thirty billion dollar settlements in the West Bank if they paid the bills from their own pockets. "Rich uncles" donate that money and/or provide soft loans. They do so because, for them, Israel belongs to the empire. In short, it serves their interests, although a small but growing number of people are beginning to realize that Israel is becoming more of a permanent liability than a strategic partner.[1]

It is not only the flow of hardware, military equipment, and advanced technology that provides the fuel to maintain the occupying power, but it is also the "software"—the culture, the narrative, and the theology—that helps to power the state of Israel. These provide the soft power or halo that enables Israel to continue to get away with its oppression of the Palestinian people without serious ramifications. This software was long in the making, but it became a dominant reality following World War II. Since then, we have been told that God is on the other side, on Israel's side. From that time on the story has been mixed with history, and biblical Israel with the modern state of Israel. The myth of a Judeo-Christian tradition has blurred the scene in Palestine, and for the last sixty-three years Palestinians have been demonized by a dominant Western culture.

DOMINANT CULTURE

When I talk about a theology and a dominant culture that provides the software and soft power for the continuing Israeli occupation, what comes to mind first is a creative type of hardline evangelical Christian.[2] Mainstream evangelical culture is based on four pillars: personal conversion, biblical literalism, involvement in mission, and a kind of millennialism that is often connected to Israel. Israel's military victory in 1967 and subsequent occupation of the West Bank, the heartland of the Bible, gave this movement a tremendous boost. Many of those who followed the news at that time thought they were experiencing divine history unfolding before them. This evangelical movement is powerful and claims, in the United States alone, to have between thirty and ninety million members. Israel theology is part and parcel of evangelical Sunday preaching and a recurrent popular theme. Indeed, Israel theology is part of its mobilizing power. Evangelicals can show a "Deus gloriosus," a victorious God who resembles the empire, and who is still active and visible in history today. This Israel theology is particularly menacing because it is not mere theology but is also a thriving business for evangelical leaders, many of whom earn their reputations as well as their bread and butter espousing such a mindset.

Surprisingly, another kind of subtle culture and theology is also in evidence in mainline Christianity. One would not necessarily expect to find it there, since this form of Christianity is a child of the Enlightenment, which is liberal and justice oriented. But here too, since World War II, interesting developments have occurred within the realm of theology. Julia O'Brien has identified four distinctive features that are characteristic of mainline Protestant hermeneutics:

> For typical U.S. mainline Protestants, an interpretation of a biblical text is convincing and compelling if they hear it as:

> - Liberal, supporting universal human rights, especially for those whom they recognize as historically oppressed, and even more especially women.
> - Scientific, objectively verified by the text itself or, even more, by historians and archaeologists.
> - Savvy, sufficiently skeptical of human bias.
> - Supportive of Judaism and supported by Jewish readers.

> An interpretation is *problematic* if they hear it as:

> - Socially conservative, unconcerned with the improvement of this world, especially the status of women.
> - Fundamentalist or overly pious, accepting biblical testimony at face value.

- Ideological, promoting only one side of a conflict that they believe is multi-faceted.
- Challenging what Jews say about the Old Testament.[3]

The danger in this liberal mainline hermeneutics is that it reflects a second stream of dominant culture and discourse in the West, the discourse constructed in the media. The notion of self-righteousness, although different from that found among evangelical Christians, is both deleterious and detrimental. In fact, the nostalgia for a biblical Israel, which is associated subconsciously with the modern state of Israel, has led to the suppression of the Palestinian narrative. In other words, Christian support of the Jewish people has led to support for the Israeli state and, therefore, indirect repression of the Palestinians.

A similar phenomenon to that of mainline Protestantism is also found among the American Jewish mainline discourse. While many American Jews were involved in the civil rights movement in the 1960s and are still highly active in defending various liberal values and causes, there is, when it comes to Israel, a profound disconnect. There is a deafening silence regarding the Israeli occupation of Palestinian land, a blind defense of Israeli policies, organized defamation campaigns against human rights activists, and threats to end dialogue with their Christian neighbors if the latter dare to raise the Palestinian question.[4] Suddenly the liberals look much like fundamentalists.

Even the Left in Europe and in North America became so enmeshed in a post-Holocaust theology that was propelled by the stream of dominant culture. From the so-called Christian Right to the Christian Left, including mainline and liberal Christians, the stage was influenced by one and the same culture, but in different ways.

This was the preeminent discourse for over forty years. From World War II to the 1980s, the Jewish-Israeli narrative, or the notion of a Judeo-Christian tradition, had a monopoly over Western dialogue and dominated, to a profound extent, Western culture.

Starting in the 1980s, however, a shift began to take place among Palestinians, as they started to regain their speech. In the Nakba of 1948, and the Naksa of 1967, Palestinians did not lose merely their land. Those traumas also took away their language, their memory, their narrative, and their ability to tell stories. The trauma made them "talk to themselves," blaming themselves and the others who didn't stand with them. In short, they were in a state of collective denial. But the 1980s witnessed a gradual recovery, and Palestinians began to speak out. They started challenging the empire not with weapons but, like their forefathers and foremothers, with their story. The 1980s also saw the Palestinians lose hope in the capacity or willingness of the Arab and Western worlds to bring about the change they so desperately desired. This led to assuming responsibility, challenging the dominant culture, and questioning the omnipresent narrative that for so long had monopolized the Western stage.

A VOICE FROM EXILE

It all began with a Palestinian Christian Protestant named Edward Said. Said was born in 1935 in Jerusalem in British Mandate Palestine. When the catastrophe or Nakba happened in 1948, most of Palestine fell into Israeli hands, and Said and his family had to flee to Egypt. (It sounds familiar and biblical.) From there he went to the United States, where he earned degrees from Princeton and Harvard specializing in English literature. In 1963, Said joined Columbia University, where he became a tenured professor; he taught there until the end of his life. In exile, like the forefathers and foremothers after the Babylonian invasion and the destruction of Jerusalem in 587 BC, Said started wrestling with the interpretation of history and the branding of the story. In 1978 he came to call this form of interpretation "Orientalism."[5] As a Palestinian living in the diaspora, one who mastered the tools of the empire, Said observed a disconnect and disparity between the Middle East he knew and the depiction of the Middle East in Western culture, which reflected a subtle and persistent bias against Arabs in general, and Muslims in particular. He saw a romanticization of the Middle East, whose images served the colonial ambitions of the Western empire. What appeared to be objective science was unraveled by Said as stereotype. In this stereotype the Orient was depicted as an irrational, weak, and feminine "other" that needed to be subjugated by the rational, strong, and masculine West. Said saw Orientalism as part and parcel of imperialism. The Western empire doesn't conquer the East by military means alone but also by ideological and cultural means.

Said, in his book *Orientalism,* was dealing mainly with literary criticism and did not tie that discipline to Palestine or to theology. Yet his theory is highly applicable to the dominant discourse of Western theology. The underlying assumption among liberal theologians is that they know; that they have seen the light (enlightenment); that they are critical, objective, open minded, and justice oriented. Although this may well be true for many issues, when it comes to the Middle East in general, and to the Palestinian issue in particular, there is a jarring disconnect. And this liberalism, alas, proves to be nothing but a fallacy. These liberal theologians might support numerous human rights causes, but not many are seen upholding the rights of the Palestinians. With their faith in objectivity, they are unable, regrettably, to see how subjective they are, while their self-righteousness keeps them from detecting their bias toward Judaism and the state of Israel. These Western theologians are not biased toward Israel because they are bad human beings but because this is what they hear, read, and see on their screens ad infinitum. Their bias against Arabs and Muslims is visceral and is one side of Orientalism. The other side is the bias toward Judaism and Israel in its relation to the Palestinians. The Judeo-Christian discourse is part of a subtle colonial ideology that looks at Islam as inferior.

Edward Said was, of course, not the only person who questioned the dominant discourse. But he is, without doubt, one of the founding figures of postcolonial studies.[6] It is interesting that the two other prominent founders hail from a Middle Eastern context: Albert Memmi in Tunisia, and Frantz Fanon in Algeria. Their theories were not applied immediately to theology but led to the development of postcolonial, racial-ethnic, minority, cultural, and many other forms of hermeneutics. These new hermeneutics started questioning the dominant colonial conversation of the empire. Greater numbers of people began listening to voices from the margin, eager to hear the "subaltern" speak and to begin to take seriously those on the underside of history. R. S. Sugirtharajah, one of the leading figures of postcolonial biblical studies, echoes the words of Said, applying them hermeneutically:

> Colonial reading can be summed up as informed by theories concerning the innate superiority of Western culture, the Western male as subject, and the natives, heathens, women, blacks, indigenous people, as the other, needing to be controlled and subjugated. It is based on desire for power/domination. . . . Colonial intentions were reinforced by the replacement of indigenous reading practices, negative representation of the "natives," and employment of exegetical strategies in the commentarial writing and hermeneutical discourses that

legitimize imperial control. The current move towards a postcolonial biblical criticism, seeks to overturn colonial assumptions.[7]

THE UPRISING OF THE PEOPLE

In the mid-1980s a number of Palestinians on the West Bank and Gaza came to the conclusion that if they did not speak for themselves, no one else would; subsequently, they decided to rise up against the empire. December 1987 saw the first Intifada or Uprising.[8] The first Intifada was important for several reasons. First, it changed to some extent the image of Israel in prevailing Western culture. The brutality the Israeli military employed against a mostly nonviolent movement became obvious not only to insiders but through mainline media internationally. Second, the image promoted in the War of 1967, where Israel was depicted as tiny David finally victorious over Goliath, started to erode. The picture seen on TV screens worldwide and over a period of time of a young Palestinian boy with a stone in his hand facing the latest model of Israeli military tank exposed a different face of Israel. For the first time some people in the West began experiencing a form of disconnect between the dominant discourse of Israel, the "one and only democratic state in the Middle East," and the images of Israel as an occupying military force. Third, the memory of the Jewish people as the ultimate victims in history began to change. The history and memory of pre–World War II Jews became inconsistent with the reality of the state of Israel after 1967. It was all too easy to see that something had changed in the intervening decades. Fourth, when the Palestinian people rose above their fear and were ready to face the empire, theologians could not stand still. They started organizing themselves and writing. Indeed several theological centers emerged in

Palestine dealing with contextual, liberation, and intercultural theologies.[9]

This period was characterized by an abundance of Palestinian theological publications by theologians from diverse denominational backgrounds, such as: Elias Chacour, Giries Khoury, Mitri Raheb, Munib Younan, Naim Ateek, Odeh Rantisi, Rafiq Khoury, Riah Abu El-Assal, Jean Zaru, Nur Masalha, and Michel Sabbah, among others.

RESPONSES FROM THE WORLD

Once the Palestinians started to raise their voices and tell their story, the world could no longer ignore them. By the early 1990s the initial responses to their cries showed the shortcomings and misuse of theology in relation to the Palestinian people.

The first and most important writing on this subject hailed from a British scholar, Keith Whitelam, under the title, *The Invention of Ancient Israel: The Silencing of Palestinian History.*[10] Writing in 1991, Whitelam argued that ancient Israel was invented and created after the image of the European nation state, thus retroactively fitting the modern state of Israel into the Iron Age. Reflecting on Whitelam's work, Ralph Broadbent observes,

> It is noteworthy that this book is unmentioned in the various accounts of the development of postcolonial biblical scholarship. This may be a historical accident or, it might be because most scholars involved in postcolonial studies have been New Testament specialists rather than Hebrew scripture scholars, or simply that the whole argument of the book was too hot to handle. Whatever the reason, Whitelam presents a long and detailed description of the ideological bias of much of what passes for Old Testament

scholarship. The book makes detailed reference to the postcolonial work of Edward Said and also the scholarship of the Indian-based Subaltern Studies Group.[11]

Many of the initial responses were from postcolonial biblical scholars, most of them living, like the Palestinians, on the margin.[12] For example, Robert Allen Warrior, a Native American, reads the biblical story through the eyes of the Canaanites.[13]

Chinese theologian Kwok Pui-lan struggles with the question: "Can I believe in a God who killed the Canaanites and who seems not to have listened to the cry of the Palestinians now for some forty years?"[14] In 1997 Michael Prior investigated and showed clearly "how the biblical account has been used to justify the conquest of land in different regions and at different periods, focusing on the Spanish and Portuguese colonization and settlement of Latin America, the white settlement in southern Africa, and the Zionist conquest and settlement in Palestine."[15]

New theological thinking also emerged in the 1990s among a few evangelical theologians including Don Wagner, Gary Burge, and Stephen Sizer. The titles of their books evince a shift from uncritical support for Israel in favor of Palestinian Christians. It was during this time that an organization was founded in the United States as the expression of this new consciousness among evangelicals under the moniker Evangelicals for Middle East Understanding. In 2010, a conference entitled "Christ at the Checkpoint," held on the West Bank, became the local articulation of this growing evangelical movement.[16]

NEW JEWISH VOICES

Jewish theological voices too started to be heard critiquing the policies of the state of Israel—Marc Ellis, perhaps, the most vocal among them.[17]

Soon other voices started to be heard from within Israel itself, but not necessarily among theologians. In 1988, on the Israeli side, there emerged the so-called new historians such as Benny Morris, Ilan Pappe, Avi Shlaim, Tom Segev, Simha Flapan, and Uri Davis who challenged the traditional myths of Israeli history, especially regarding Israel's role in the Palestinian Nakba of 1948. Their research became highly crucial for post-Zionist political ideology. After the first Intifada, Israeli human rights activists also began to observe and record the violations of the Israeli occupation of the Palestinians. One of them, Uri Davis, described Israel in 1987 as already "an apartheid state."[18]

Moreover, in 2009, Jewish historian Shlomo Sand of Tel Aviv University published *The Invention of the Jewish People,* showing how Jewish Intellectuals in Germany, influenced by European nationalism, embarked on a project of retroactively inventing a modern Jewish people, where "Judaism would no longer be a rich and diverse religious civilization" but rather became "an ancient people or race that was uprooted from its homeland in Canaan and arrived in its youth at the gates of Berlin."[19] Sand argues that for a number of Zionist ideologues, the mythical perception of the Jews as an ancient people led to truly racist thinking. In 2012, a second book by Sand showed how the concept of a Jewish homeland was invented by evangelical Christians together with Jewish Zionists to facilitate the colonization of Palestine.[20] Sand stands in continuity with Whitelam. What the latter tried to show for Old Testament scholarship, Sand illuminates as part of racial and political nineteenth-century European history.

QUESTIONING THE PREVAILING NARRATIVE

Most of these writings, unfortunately, did not become mainline reading matter and remained marginal. However, a few mainline theologians started questioning the "naivete" with which they were doing theology, as if it were divorced from time, space, and power centers. A good example of this shift can be seen in the work of the well-known American theologian Walter Brueggemann. In 1977, Brueggemann published *The Land*, a typical book about biblical theology in which one cannot find any mention of the peoples of the land or of their identities.[21] He and other mainstream theologians wrote about the land as if (according to the Zionist legend) it were "a land without a people for a people without a land." In the preface of the second edition of that same book, Brueggemann discussed five major developments in Old Testament Studies that needed (in 2002) to be taken into account which were not on his horizon at the time of his initial scholarship in 1979.[22] One of them was

> the recognition that the claim of "promised land" in the Old Testament is not an innocent theological claim, but is a vigorous ideological assertion on an important political scale. This insight is a subset of ideology critique in the field that has emerged as a major enterprise only in the last decades. Perhaps the most important articulation in this matter is the recognition of Jon Levenson that Israel's tradition demonizes and dismisses the Canaanites as a parallel to the anti-Semitism that is intrinsic to the New Testament. That is, Israel's text proceeds on the basis of the primal promises of Genesis 12—36 to assume entitlement to the land without regard to any other inhabitants including those who may have been there prior to Israel's emergence. . . . The shortcoming in my book reflects my inadequate understanding at that time, but also reflects the status of most Old Testament studies at that time that were still

innocently credulous about the theological importance
of the land tradition in the Old Testament. . . . Most recently scholarly attention has been given to the ongoing
ideological force (and cost) of the claim of "promised
land." On the one hand, this ideology of land entitlement . . . has served the ongoing territorial ambitions
of the state of Israel, ambitions that, as I write [April
2002], are enacted in unrestrained violence against the
Palestinian population.[23]

What Brueggemann did was to unveil the national Israeli
agenda behind the religious packaging. The native peoples of
the land—the Canaanites and the Palestinians—were identified by Brueggemann by name, and the suffering done to them
under religious pretext was finally highlighted.

When we look at these theological developments, there are
several noteworthy points to be observed:

- The first signs of a "theological awakening" regarding
  Palestine were visible across the theological landscape
  and included evangelical, mainstream, liberal, and Jewish theologians.
- Second, the theologians in this era, like Palestinian
  theologians at that time, did not question the theological discourse itself, but only its ethical side. For many of
  them, more subconsciously than consciously, the modern
  state of Israel stood in some continuity to biblical Israel.
  The only problem they saw was that the modern state
  of Israel was not as innocent as they had thought. Israel
  does not "behave biblically," is not "pursuing justice," and
  is not adhering to its "calling and election."
- Third, almost all of them, except Whitelam, saw in the Canaanites the prototype of the contemporary Palestinians.

Even Palestinian theologians and supporters of their cause have internalized Western discourse. They recognize the injustice they have experienced, but at the end of the day, they identify them with the Canaanites. Clearly, they have been mixing the biblical story, as such, with political history. Let me illustrate this with two personal recollections.

A few years ago, at the inauguration of a new building that was supposed to be used for Christian-Jewish dialogue in the Bethlehem region, a German Reformed pastor and one of the main sponsors of that building stood in the pulpit to declare how happy he was to be able to come from Germany to bring the children of Isaac and the children of Ishmael together after four thousand years of hostility. From his voice one could sense that he was serious about what he was preaching and that he felt that he and his group were called to a noble, historic, and divine mission. The Germans and internationals in that church service were in tears, as they understood themselves to be seeing salvation history unfold before their eyes. I, however, was in total shock and grew increasingly furious and disturbed.

Who, for heaven's sake, was this German pastor to think himself a mediator, a third category over and above Isaac and Ishmael? And what kind of exegesis was he preaching where he switched from the time of Isaac to the present as if there were not four thousand years of history in between, as if history had been on hold and frozen just waiting for this new messenger to show up and complete that which was incomplete? And how utterly naive to mix the biblical story with history without reflecting on its contexts and shifting identities! For this German pastor it was a given that I, as a Palestinian, was a descendant of Ishmael, and that the three Jewish rabbis sitting in the front of the sanctuary were the children of Isaac. He had traveled from Germany to bring us together and to make peace between us. Many German congregations were so moved by the vision that this pastor espoused that they raised over two million dollars for it. The pastor obviously felt very good about such a response and about himself, and was proud to be entrusted with such a mission. While listening to him, I wondered who told him that I saw myself as the descendant of Ishmael? And who said that the three Jewish rabbis were Isaac's children? What was he talking about? Was he referring to race, ethnicity, religion, or . . . something else? And if those three Jewish rabbis were considered descendants of Isaac, and I a descendant of Ishmael, then who was he, as a German Christian?

I also remember vividly a discussion I once had with an American woman. While conversing with me about the situation of the Palestinians in the West Bank, she looked at me and said, "I don't understand why Israel is not adhering to the Bible. God told them very clearly to 'take care of the strangers.'" It was clear that she was referring to several passages in the Bible, such as Exodus 22:21 and 23:9. I could tell that this woman had good intentions. She was truly unhappy with the way we, as Palestinians, are treated by the Israeli occupation. And yet, I was angry. I replied:

"This is exactly the problem. Because the most important question is: Who is the stranger here? Is it I, the Palestinian and native of this land, whose ancestors have been living here for centuries, or is it the Israeli settlers being imported from Russia and Ethiopia to ensure a Jewish demographic majority over the Arab population? I'm not the stranger here! Nor are my people! We belong to this land more than anyone else. We were made strangers."

This is precisely the crux of the problem: the natives of the land have been made strangers in order to make room for an invented people to occupy the land.

These two stories are highly representative and typical of what we face as Palestinians in general and as Palestinian Christians in particular when dealing with Christians and non-Christians acquainted with the biblical narratives. On the one hand, we are viewed as the Canaanites or as the descendants of Ishmael, which means that theologically we are inferiors and politically second-class citizens. Ishmael then gets connected to Arabs and Muslims, who are viewed with an Orientalist lens, and, after 9/11, with fear and hatred, as well. On the other hand, our history, our roots, and our presence in the Holy Land are glaringly overlooked so that we become aliens and strangers, and this by divine order.

In his *Short Introduction to Hermeneutics,* David Jasper writes:

> What can hermeneutics, as we have been studying it, contribute to the *ethical* dilemmas posed when texts and of power become texts of terror? Can we stand neutral, as merely "academic" interpreters? Is hermeneutics necessarily a political activity? We need to be aware that such a pernicious political program as apartheid in South Africa had its beginnings in a particular biblical hermeneutics that saw all things created as distinct under God, their differences to be clearly acknowledged. . . . We might also recall that apartheid in South Africa arose, to some extent at least, from biblical criticism and interpretation. In the postcolonial era of the present day it is easy to see how a very difficult hermeneutic pertains, and how not only is the Bible to be read in different way in the light of political and social experience, but the power of the new reader must be turned against old prejudices that were once regarded as unquestioned truths.[24]

PROMISING DEVELOPMENTS

With the turn of the millennium, three promising new developments occurred in various academic disciplines that will, in the long term, question the prevailing narrative.

The first development was the emergence of empire studies. What began with a primary focus on the British Empire was widened in scope after the war on Iraq to consider the American Empire. These developments made imperial studies hermeneutically relevant, and many US theologians, including Richard A. Horsley, Warren Carter, and Walter Brueggemann, turned with renewed interest to the study of empire in relation to the Old and New Testaments.

Still, none of them dared to apply the lessons of imperial studies to consideration of the state of Israel. Although most of these studies were done by biblical scholars, many of them were applying what they learned about the Roman Empire to the American Empire. They talk about biblical Israel facing different empires, but they fail to make the connection from there to the modern Middle East, connecting the empire with the modern state of Israel, and the Palestinians with biblical Israel. In fact, only one Western theologian, and in one sentence, made that association. In his article, "Early Israel as an Anti-Imperial Community," Norman Gottwald paints a highly idealistic picture of ancient Israel. But then he concludes, "In a supreme irony, Palestinians of the West Bank may most nearly approximate the early Israelites since they occupy the same terrain, practice similar livelihoods, and long for deliverance from the 'Canannite' state of Israel backed by the American Empire."[25]

The second development was the emergence of a whole new field of study devoted to Christian Zionism that started showing how dangerous such an ideology is.[26]

The third interesting development in recent years has been the work on Jesus and cultural complexity. In his essay on the present debate about the historical Jesus, James G. Crossley investigates

> the role of the claim that "Jesus was a Jew" in light of modern discussions of identity and its construction. . . . Crossley situates the discussion of the Jewish Jesus within the political context after the 1967 war between Israel and the neighboring Arab states. Crossley sees that war as a major turning point toward a very pro-Israel political attitude in the United States, the UK, and other European countries, and he finds that this attitude strongly influences scholarly perspectives in Jesus Studies. The implicit presuppositions of most historical Jesus Studies, he argues, are pro-Israel and anti-Arab and Palestinians. Crossley showed clearly "how New Testament and Christian origins scholarship is profoundly influenced by and supportive of contemporary Anglo-American power."[27]

This thesis was investigated further by Halvor Moxnes, who shows how the rise of nationalism in Europe and the beginnings of the historical Jesus studies in the nineteenth century identified Jesus and Christianity "with national identities and with Western colonialism and imperialism."[28]

KAIROS PALESTINE

One last important development in recent years should be mentioned in this context, that is, the Kairos Palestine document entitled "A Moment of Truth." Written by a Palestinian Christian group of theologians and lay leaders from different denominations in 2009, the document challenges the churches in the West "to revisit theologies that justify crimes perpetrated against our (Palestinian) people and the dispossession of the land."[29] In this historic document the Palestinian Christian writers declare "that the military occupation of our land is a sin against God and humanity, and that any theology that legitimizes the occupation is far from Christian teachings."[30] The reception that the document received worldwide showed that a shift is happening in the West as well as the South regarding Palestine. This document shows a new stamina and a renewed energy within the Palestinian Christian community. Yet, it stopped short of adopting a genuine Palestinian Christian narrative that looks at history *longue durée*. In what follows I hope to build on these recent developments by applying new methodologies to the Palestinian context, thus creating a new theological discourse in Palestine.

3

The Geo-Politics of the Middle East

I'm often invited to speak about issues related to the so-called Middle East. I like to commence these occasions by stating that this is terminology that sounds obvious, as if everyone knows what we are talking about, and yet it is a misleading. The question to pose is: middle of where and east of what? Once this question is asked, people realize that we are dealing with a Eurocentric view of the world. Only by looking at our region of the planet from Europe does one see it as east/ southeast. To distinguish it from the Far East, Europeans first called it the Near East and later the Middle East.

It is noteworthy that the term was coined in the mid-nineteenth century when Europe was at the height of its power. The region's name is thus closely related to imperial power. The use of the term became widespread only after the collapse of a vast Ottoman Empire that had held the region together for hundreds of years. The designation of the Middle East is therefore part and parcel of the colonial history of the region. "Reconceptualizing the Orient as the Near/Middle East and Far East vis-à-vis Europe reaffirmed the central position of Europe in this imagery and further peripheralized the East, Europe being the metropolis."[1] "The idea of the Middle East cannot be separated from the power to create and impose categories of knowledge on the rest of the world. The Middle East exists because the West has possessed sufficient power to give the idea substance. In this regard the colonial past and the imperial present are parts of the equation that make the Middle East real."[2]

But behind this name is not just a colonial perspective but an intrinsic identity question. The Middle East is not easy to pinpoint, because it has no clear definition or boundaries. While to some and in certain contexts it once meant the whole of the area from India in the east to Morocco in the west, and from Turkey in the north to Sudan in the south, it is understood today more or less as the area covering the Arabian Gulf to the east, and Syria and Iraq to the north, encompassing Egypt in the west, and as far south as the Sudan.

One important feature of the Middle East is that it has no "middle" or center. Rather, it has different centers of power separated by deserts and/or mountain chains.

Geographically speaking, part of the Middle East is located in Asia, but part is also found in North Africa. In fact, the bulk of the Middle East could be called West Asia. This is the term used, for example, at the United Nations. The other portion is still referred to as North Africa.

Historically speaking, and for over a millennium, from Alexander the Great in the fourth century BC to Charlemagne in the eight century AD, the nexus of the region was located to the west, where the Mediterranean was the center and the region became part of "Europe." The rise of Islam and its spread throughout the Middle East pulled the region away from Europe's sphere of influence, making it part of the Arab-Islamic world.

Religiously speaking, the region changed religion at least four times, from "paganism" to Judaism, to Christianity, to Islam. Because of these not inconsiderable realities, the region was incapable of self-definition and thus the prevailing empires imposed their *weltpolitik*.

But let's go back in history to the times when the region assumed its major contours.

"The city-state was the primary political element from 3000 to approximately 1600."[3] And the Middle East was full of them.

> From 1500 to 1200 all the regions of the Near East went through a cycle of creation, fluorescence, and fall of centralized states. There were at least five zones where political unification and centralization of power took place, followed by a period of prosperity that ended in rather sudden collapse. In four of those zones the entire period can be studied as the history of one state: the Middle Elamite Kingdom in western Iran, Kassite Babylonia in southern Mesopotamia, the Hittite New Kingdom in Anatolia (a state called Hatti by its contemporaries), and New Kingdom Egypt in North Africa. In Northern Mesopotamia two district states dominated in succession, Mittani and Assyria.[4]

The first empire to develop in the Middle East was Assyria, starting in the mid-ninth century BC and ending in 612, followed by Babylon from 612 until 539, then Persia from mid-sixth century to 331 BC.

It is not the norm to begin a theological book with geopolitics. That is not the way I was educated. Yet over a period of years I began to see religion as the default response to the geo-politics of the region. I hope that this book will show why.

A close look at the history of the region shows that as early as the fourth millennium BC the nucleus for two major centers of powers had evolved. Their development was tightly connected to geography. At one end there is the Nile and on the other two rivers: the Tigris and Euphrates. Around these waters the two major states of the region evolved in the middle of the second millennium to later become the two major regional empires controlling the region: Egypt in the West, and Mesopotamia in the East. Throughout history Egypt and Mesopotamia developed as the poles of the region. This is where the critical masses were in terms of numbers, and this is where civilization accumulated knowledge and power. Most of the time the seat of the political and religious leadership switched between the two poles. Even today, those two centers, Egypt and Syria/Iraq, although greatly weakened, continue to be important players in the Middle East.

But they never were and still are not the only players in the region; nor did they develop in a vacuum. At approximately the same time and in close proximity three other regional powers were developing on the boundaries of the region, engulfing it from three sides. These three powers surround the Middle East even today and determine to a good extent what happens. There is Persia/Iran to the east, Turkey to the north, and Europe to the west. A look at the history of the Middle East shows that these three powers greatly determined the history and politics of the region. There are only a few and isolated exceptions, where other powers came to control the Middle East, such as the Moguls in the sixteenth century.

Studying the history of the region of the last three millennia shows that the Middle East was always controlled by one of these five empires, albeit with different names, constellations, and degrees of power. Often the Middle East was under the influence of more than one power fighting for ultimate control. In that sense one can say that the Middle East is best described as being in the middle of empires.

This was, in fact, largely the case until the mid-twentieth century, when new players became involved in the region. In 1948, with the creation of the State of Israel, an exception to the above-mentioned rule emerged: a small country with few natural resources and a tiny population developed into a regional power, albeit by proxy. Israel today can be seen as the last chapter of Western colonialism. The United States and, to a lesser extent, Russia, are a second exception to the rule. As the world's two superpowers they held great sway in the region and beyond in the Cold War era. With the end of the Cold War the only remaining superpower was the United States. A third exception and yet other new and unexpected players in the Middle East are Saudi Arabia and Qatar, thanks to the influence of the petro-dollar.

These three factors, the United States, Israel, and oil characterize the politics of the Middle East in the twenty-first century. The historical regional powers of Egypt, Syria, Iran, and Turkey currently seem to be weak. Egypt, Iraq, and Syria are experiencing great internal turmoil, while Iran is under economic siege. And with the absence of a united European foreign policy and a threatened euro, the actual influence of Europe in the Middle East is limited. Turkey appears to be the only one of the five traditional regional powers to be preparing once again to assume a major role in the region.

4

Palestine

THE IMAGE

Ancient maps of the Middle East always show Palestine at the center. This is the case in the mosaic map of the city of Madaba in Jordan dating from the sixth century. The map covers the area from present-day south Lebanon to Egypt, with the Old City of Jerusalem at its center. On another map Palestine is located at the center of three continents; Asia, Africa, and Europe are depicted as three leaves representing three continents held together by a center that is Jerusalem. In the Church of the Holy Sepulchre and in the middle of the Greek Orthodox church known as Catholicon, the spot is referred to as "the navel of the earth," making the point that Jerusalem is the epic center of the world.

This might be true religiously, as I will explain later, but politically it is nothing but a myth. Interestingly, the land Palestine/Israel has a grand ideological reputation that does not correspond in any way to its actual size, geographic location, or geo-political role. The media attention that Palestine receives today is in no way proportionate to its actual political standing, which is why in large part there is so much tension and disparity between the many political efforts invested in "peace talks" and actual solving of the conflict. Palestine might be "holy," but it is certainly not "oily." Ending the Iraqi occupation of Kuwait in 1991 took only one UN resolution and several months of negotiation, while ending the Israeli occupation of the West Bank and Gaza is still pending. This tension is even more pronounced if one reflects on the countless prayers lifted for the peace of Jerusalem worldwide and the absence of peace in Jerusalem throughout history. To understand this phenomenon, we must again look at Palestine from a geo-political perspective.

THE GEO-POLITICS

Historic Palestine, the land between the Jordan River to the east, the Mediterranean to the west, the Negev Desert to the south, and Mount Hermon to the north, has a unique and intriguing position in the region. The land is isolated by three natural barriers: water, deserts, and mountains. And yet the land is found at the crossroads of three continents, forming a bridge, and thus is anything but isolated.

A Buffer Zone

It can be argued that Palestine is located, at least geographically, in the heart of the Middle East, but that does not necessarily make it the center. The opposite, in fact, is true. Palestine is a land at the periphery. As early as the second millennium BC, when the five major powers of the region were developing, Palestine did not possess the clout to join the "club of five." Indeed, Palestine became the place where the different magnetic fields of the regional powers would collide.

> During the centuries from 1500 to 1200 the Near East became fully integrated in an international system that involved the entire region from western Iran to the Aegean Sea, from Anatolia to Nubia. A number of large

territorial states interacted with one another as equals and rivals. Located between them, especially in the Syro-Palestinian area, was a set of smaller states that owed allegiance to their more powerful neighbors, and which were often used as proxies in their competition.[1]

The influence of the regional powers over Palestine made it a buffer zone. Palestine was often the distance each of the empires needed from the others to feel secure or the red line that no other power should cross. In reality, and geo-politically, Palestine is, in fact, nothing but a land on the margins. Contrary to its religious reputation and geographical location, in reality and geo-politically the land lies on the periphery of the Fertile Crescent and is a borderland for diverse empires.

A Battlefield

Situated between different empires, the fertile plains of Palestine often became the most suitable battlefield to keep wars and their tragedies away from the heartland of those empires. It is no coincidence that Armageddon was envisioned as taking place in the most fertile and largest plain of Palestine. This wasn't a revealed vision of the end times, but it corresponded to the political reality of the region. Wars constitute reality in Palestine. I know this not merely from history books but from my own experience. I am just fifty years old and have already lived through nine wars.

Occupied

While regional powers were satisfied with Palestine as a buffer zone, a buffer was not enough once a power became an empire. Empires were totalitarian in their understanding and wanted to control not just Palestine but any country in the region they could. Due to geo-political positioning between powers, Palestine has mainly been an occupied land—occupied by the Egyptians, Assyrians, Babylonians, Persians, Greeks, Romans, Arabs, Crusaders, Ottomans, British, and Israelis.

I have a friend who wanted to take an oath not to visit Palestine as long as it is occupied—in this case by Israel. I told him that such a stance means he has decided never to visit Palestine. For when in the last three thousand years has Palestine not been occupied? Sadly, it seems as if Palestine and occupation are synonymous. Historically, Occupied Palestine has unfortunately been the norm. There are a few exceptions for short periods: the Davidic State at the turn of the first millennium BC (although this might be a myth); the Hasmonite Kingdom, 164–63 BC; the Kingdom of Herod the Great, 34–4 BC (although this was part and parcel of the Roman Empire); and the Daher El-Omar reign, AD 1690–1775, to name a few. But even those were more akin to tolerated self-rule than states in the real sense of the term.

Divided

A close look at historic maps of Palestine reveals that the land was unified as one entity mainly when it was occupied. If not completely occupied, Palestine sometimes stood in the influence sphere of two of the five powers simultaneously, which led naturally to having the land divided into two or more entities. This was the case, for example, when the Assyrians occupied the northern part of Palestine, stopping north of Ramallah in order not to be too close to Egypt's sphere of influence in the south. But there were also a few exceptions when a political vacuum occurred in the region. Whenever such a political vacuum became a reality, a slight chance existed to declare independence, but the native peoples of the land, left to themselves, always had difficulty in maintaining their unity. Even during times of rare self-determination, internal fighting was more the rule than the exception. The biblical narrative reveals that the struggle among the different groups within the land—Judeans, Israelites, Philistines, and Jebusites—required most of David's attention. The fact that after Solomon the land was divided yet again shows that the Davidic Kingdom was not significant. After the Assyrian occupation two different identities developed in Palestine: one in the northern part, where the people became Samaritans; and another in the south, where the people became Judeans. After the death of Herod the Great the land was divided among his sons. Something similar happened after the death of Daher El-Omar. This was true too after 1948, when the State of Israel was established on 77 percent of historic Palestine, while the rest was subdivided in such a way that Jordan was brought into the West Bank, and Egypt into the Gaza Strip.

The geography of the land added another reason for territorial in-fighting and instability: the land is surrounded by semi-desert on two sides. And it was to the deserts that most of the Zealots and fighters retreated to escape the persecution of the occupier. Yet at the same time, these groups and various Bedouin tribes terrorized the populated city centers of Palestine, preventing any accumulation of power or culture or civilization to blossom. The Bedouin tribes infiltrated the mountains, and the mountain people in turn slowly infiltrated the coastal areas. The deserts thus developed over and against the mountains, and the mountains against the sea.[2]

In looking at these salient features of Palestine past and present, one sees how the geo-politics of the region determines the fate of this land, a fate that is very difficult to escape. Being largely an occupied land, liberation from occupation is a central theme throughout history and plays a major role in the Bible. Yet, maintaining control of the land and promoting the unity of its peoples remain an uphill struggle. In short, it is not possible to understand the meaning or importance of liberation and community without some knowledge and awareness of the geo-political standing of Palestine.

5

The Empire

The first decade of the twenty-first century saw an increase in the number of studies related to the issue of empire. A marked increase is especially evident after the war in Iraq. Many were by American theologians critical of their own government's policies. Although the United States plays a strategic role in the Middle East today, I would like to concentrate this chapter on the State of Israel as the expression of the empire in Palestine, knowing that this approach might be shocking because of the religious overtones made to the State of Israel through Judaism.

Empires develop similar theologies, policies, and tactics. They inherit policies, refine them, and pass those policies on from one empire to the next. While each empire remains singular, it is still possible to identify similar patterns in most imperial contexts. In the case of Palestine these themes have been played repeatedly throughout history and are still being heard today. I would like to touch briefly on seven of these patterns.

CONTROL OF MOVEMENT

Empires are always about control. Control is seen as necessary to securing the movement of people related to the empire, its soldiers, and its routes. Watch towers, military fortresses, and checkpoints are vivid expressions of this obsession with security. Herod was keen on control, as were the Crusaders, the British, and the Israelis. The people of Palestine over the centuries have been exposed to all of these control mechanisms. And yet, there was never a system like the present Israeli one, which is trying to confine the native people of Palestine in geographical pockets with little choice of movement. Gaza is 360 square miles surrounded by walls and seas, making it the biggest open-air prison in the world to date. Palestinians from Gaza cannot travel to visit Palestinians in the West Bank. Agricultural products from Gaza are not allowed to enter the West Bank or Israel or even to be shipped to Europe. The West Bank, for its part, looks very much like a piece of Swiss cheese, where Israel gets the cheese—the land and its resources—while pushing the Palestinians into the holes. Each of the holes, or cities, is controlled by a checkpoint. Palestinians can't travel from any major city to another without crossing an Israeli military checkpoint. There are over 522 Israeli checkpoints and roadblocks within the West Bank, separating farmers from their land, children from their schools, and family members from one another.[1] Movement into Israel is prohibited for almost all Palestinians as only a tiny percentage of Palestinians have a permit to enter Israel. And then there is the 443–mile-long wall that sneaks deep into the West Bank like an ugly snake putting prime land into Israeli hands.[2]

Empires do not control only the native people they rule; they also work to ensure that visitors coming in contact with the land and its native people are controlled. In 2010, evangelical preacher Tony Campolo attended a theological conference in Bethlehem. Upon arrival at Ben Gurion Airport in Tel Aviv, Israeli officials told him that they would like to invite him for a cup of coffee in their offices and have a chat. For almost four hours he was questioned about his decision to attend a conference in Bethlehem, what he thought of the Kairos Palestine document, and how he knew some of these "radical" Palestinian theologians. This was supposed to be VIP treatment. Others who are part of solidarity movements are often detained at the airport and sent back to their home countries. When this highly reputed American evangelical preacher related his story, I told him, "Welcome to Palestine. As someone who knows his Bible well you should not have been surprised by such treatment. The same VIP treatment was also extended to the magi from the East who came to see Jesus in Bethlehem. Herod too invited them 'for a cup of coffee' to ascertain why they wanted to travel to Bethlehem, and how they knew about that newborn child. So now you have experienced something biblical. Welcome to the Holy Land!" I still recall how everyone in the group laughed. Then an American woman attending the conference asked me, "So what should we tell the Israelis at the airport when they question us about where we have been? What should we say?" I replied: "I wish I could tell you what the angel told the magi, after visiting Jesus; basically showing them another route not controlled by the Roman soldiers. Unfortunately, all roads, airports, and borders are controlled by Israel. By the way, an invitation to drink a cup of coffee by Israeli or Arab intelligence authorities is known in political jargon as interrogation."

CONTROL OF RESOURCES

For an empire to expand, it needs to control the natural resources of conquered countries and to utilize them for the betterment of the empire rather than for the benefit of the native peoples. The technological development of the empire is used to maximize the exploitation of those resources. A good example in Palestinian history has been the control of water. For the expansion of Jerusalem under Herod, greater

Jerusalem was in need of vast amounts of water. Jerusalem has no natural springs except for a small spring called Siloa. Herod utilized Roman technology and the cheap labor provided by the native peoples to create long aqueduct lines to collect the water from the Bethlehem/Hebron area in the south of Palestine and bring it to Jerusalem. If one looks at the locations of the newly established cities and fortresses in Palestine during the Roman, Byzantine, and Crusader periods, it is evident that cities were built in relation to the availability of water.

The control of water under Israeli occupation is a continuation of this imperial natural resource strategy.[3] Israel uses over 80 percent of the natural water resources of the West Bank, leaving only 20 percent to the native Palestinians. But water is still fully controlled by Israel. The locations of Israeli settlements in the West Bank are established upon the land's natural aquifers. A close look at where the wall is being built shows that its location has less to do with "security concerns" and more with a massive land-and-water grab. As of the writing of this book, the Palestinian Authority has no authority over the water and natural resources in the West Bank. Both are still under direct Israeli military control. The Palestinian Authority is not even permitted to dig for water in the small "Area A" pockets it controls. Significantly, the amount of water available to an Israeli settler in the West Bank is four times that available to a Palestinian. The same is true for stones, minerals, agricultural land, and archaeological sites in the West Bank, much of which is under direct Israeli control.[4]

SETTLEMENTS

A highly important aspect of the matrix of control that empires exercise is the construction of new colonies or settlements or cities built on conquered land with the express purpose of controlling the native people and all natural resources.

The gigantic administrative apparatus of the empire and its financial means are directed toward these building activities. While native villages and cities grow and evolve naturally over time and at a "normal" speed, settlements are established strategically and deliberately to control. Local villages and towns are built at the foot of hills to provide natural protection from weather and, at the same time, not to use valuable farmland; settlements, in contrast, are erected either on the top of hills, at cross-roads, or next to natural resources, providing the maximum level of control. The Greeks, Romans, Byzantines, Crusaders, and Ottomans each had extensive settlement projects.

Yet the State of Israel has exceeded all of them when it comes to settlement activities.[5] The building frenzy began in the late nineteenth century with small, mainly agricultural, settlements, and continued after 1948 and after 1967, becoming a powerful and prime tool to control the whole of historic Palestine from the Mediterranean to the Jordan River, from Dan to Eilat. Israeli settlements follow the same imperial pattern.[6] They too are built on hilltops, psychologically "looking down" upon Palestinians. They are constructed as a chain, intentionally creating connectivity for Israeli settlers while, at the same time, disconnecting Palestinian towns and villages. And they are placed strategically next to natural and cultural resources in order to exploit the resources of the country to expand the empire. The Israeli settlement activity in the West Bank has made the aim of establishing a Palestinian state a de facto impossibility. Ongoing settlement activity since the Oslo Accords has sabotaged any potential two-state solution or a viable peace settlement with the Palestinians. The presence of almost half a million settlers in the West Bank, their interdependence upon the Israeli military, and their attitude of superiority toward the local Palestinian population they have displaced is making territorial compromise null and void.

STATE TERROR

The word *terror* is usually reserved for those military guerrilla groups fighting the empire, whose use of language and word selection is often controlled by the empire. While the empire utilizes the most violent means to suppress the native people, this is seldom described in terms of terrorism but as the empire "bringing civilization" to the uncivilized. Destruction of whole villages, the execution of hundreds of people, and the torture of thousands more are all means used by the empire regularly and over decades with the aim of subjugating the native peoples to ensure that they will reach a point where they will not even dare to think of resisting the empire.

Israel is following the same pattern. Four hundred eighteen Palestinian villages were completely destroyed in 1948 to make the areas where Jews were to settle "clean of Arabs."[7] The massacre in the village of Deir Yassin by Jewish terror groups was meant to spread great fear and trauma among the Palestinian inhabitants, thus forcing them to leave.[8] The number of Palestinians imprisoned just in the West Bank and the Gaza strip since 1967 is in the hundreds of thousands, with over forty-seven hundred political prisoners currently still held in Israeli prisons.[9] But Israeli state terror is not merely confined to Palestine and the Palestinians. Internationally, the State of Israel, through its powerful lobbies, succeeds in silencing voices that would dare to criticize its policies, theology, or narrative—including Jewish voices. Critical Jewish voices are ousted from their communities, fired from their jobs, and described as "self-hating Jews." International politicians, theologians, and human rights activists who dare to question the official Israeli state narrative are labeled anti-Semitic, making this title the modern form of public execution, ending their prospective careers, and destroying their reputations, so that no one dares to repeat such an action. Self-censorship becomes a powerful method of silencing people. Mild forms of "critique light" are permitted. And for opportunistic scholars who worship the empire, praising the Israeli state and propagating the supremacy of the Judeo-Christian narrative is a way to help shape their career paths and climb the ladder. Jesus faced similar temptation in the desert when offered the glory of the empire: "All these I will give you, if you will fall down and worship me" (Mt 4:9). Jesus resisted this temptation and had to pay a bitter price: crucifixion.

EXILE

Exile is another pivotal pattern found in empire. In many cases a strategy of conquering exists to drive people out of their country. This is sometimes done aggressively and violently as part of a racial-religious ethnic cleansing policy that leads to mass deportation. Sometimes it is done passively as people, in fear for their lives, flee conflict zones. In many cases the empire doesn't allow those deportees or refugees to return to their homelands. The only hope left for those forced to live in exile is a regime change which means a change of the empire. At the time of the Babylonian invasion the theme of exile was a prime example. Phenomenologically this is a common global pattern.[10]

In 1948, when the State of Israel was created, the destruction of villages and the terror tactics of the Jewish Haganah and Irgun groups were major factors in driving Palestinians out of their homeland and forcing tens of thousands to flee in fear for their lives.[11] Within only a few months, approximately 750,000 Palestinian refugees lost their homes, land, and access to their belongings.[12] In some cases, like Iqrit and Birem, even after the end of the war Palestinians were asked to leave their villages for a transitional period with the promise of being allowed to return. Yet, they were never allowed back. There are nineteen Palestinian refugee camps in the West Bank; over two-thirds of the Palestinians in the Gaza Strip are refugees; and there are thirty-one Palestinian refugee camps in Jordan, Lebanon, and Syria, making the five million Palestinian refugees the largest refugee population worldwide. These refugees are denied the right to return or any monetary compensation requested by United Nations resolutions. The Palestinians are the only group of people globally who have a permanent committee at the United Nations (the Relief and Works Agency) designated to deal with this particular issue.

JERUSALEM AND THE TEMPLE

In contexts of war national capitals and major religious shrines are of strategic significance. The destruction of the capital city and important shrines is viewed as a sign of the capitulation of the occupied. The victory of the empire is seen as underlining the supremacy of the god of the empire, while the attack on the symbols of power, sovereignty, unity, identity, and dignity of the occupied people is perceived as a sign of a weak god. It is not surprising that Jerusalem was destroyed by the Babylonians, Romans, and Persians and that the Temple was repeatedly set on fire. The Babylonians destroyed it in 587 BC and the Romans in AD 70. The Persians destroyed the Byzantine Church of the Holy Sepulchre in AD 614. In 1969, Denis Michael Rohen, a "crazy" Australian evangelical Christian, tried to set al Aqsa mosque on fire. Today, several Jewish religious fanatics are trying to dig under, beneath, and around this mosque hoping either to destroy it or to gain control of it, as they did at the Ibrahimi Mosque in Hebron. In other contexts temples are not necessarily destroyed but are transformed to become temples of the imperial god. This was the case with the Greeks and Crusaders. The transformation of the Church of Hagia Sophia in Istanbul (formerly Constantinople) into a mosque and later into a museum is a vivid example of such a strategy.

In July 2000, during the so-called Camp David Summit among President Clinton, President Arafat, and Prime Minister Barak, the lectionary text provided for the Sunday the leaders met was from the Isaiah 40:1–9. There was a great deal of hope invested in those negotiations, and many thought that a peace deal was around the corner. Unfortunately, the summit ultimately proved to be a total failure, leading to the escalation of the conflict and the end of any serious peace negotiations. The propaganda machinery of the empire blamed Arafat, as it is always easier to blame the victim. But the negotiations collapsed over three issues: the right of return of Palestinian refugees, the question of Jerusalem, and the control over the area around the al Aqsa mosque. It was striking for me to read Isaiah 40:1–9 in that particular context:

> Comfort, O comfort my people,
>   says your God.
> Speak tenderly to Jerusalem,
>   and cry to her
> that she has served her term,
>   that her penalty is paid,
> that she has received from the LORD's hand
>   double for all her sins.
>
> A voice cries out:
> "In the wilderness prepare the way of the
>   LORD
>   make straight in the desert a highway for
>   our God. . . .
>
> Get you up to a high mountain,
>   O Zion, herald of good tidings;

lift up your voice with strength,
  O Jerusalem, herald of good tidings,
  lift it up, do not fear;
say to the cities of Judah,
  "Here is your God!"

The three important issues for Isaiah in the post-exilic, post-Babylonian context were the return from Exile, Jerusalem, and the Temple (Zion). The three issues that led to the collapse of the Camp David Summit were almost the same. Clinton had the opportunity to be like Cyrus, facilitating the return of Palestinian refugees, but he failed. Creating a new template of sharing Jerusalem rather than disputing it failed as well. Currently, Israel is actively seeking to confine Arab East Jerusalem in order to be the sole arbiter over the city and to prevent the establishment of a Palestinian state—in short, to have a total monopoly. The efforts to gain control of al Aqsa will thus only intensify in the future.

IMPERIAL THEOLOGY

Empires can't survive by their military, political, and economic power and might alone. Rather, the justification of the empire has to be based on a higher logic; the violation of human rights needs to have something akin to divine purpose and to be set within an ideological and theological framework.[13] This was true for the Roman Empire, which believed it was destined to bring world peace through dominion. It was true of the Byzantine Empire, which, with the ecumenical creed, tried to glue its territories and identities together. It was true for the Crusaders, who believed they were present to cleanse the Holy Land from the infidels. It was also the raison d'être for the Muslim Empire, which believed it was bringing the world out of the age of ignorance *(jahiliyah)*.

In modern colonial history, in a similar vein, empires justified their expansion and subordination of other lands and peoples under the cover of bringing civilization, enlightenment, and progress to people living in darkness and backwardness.

Israel is no exception. From day one, theology has provided the narrative glue that keeps Israeli society together. Even for secular Jews this narrative became foundational. Atheist Jews might not believe in God, but they may well believe that God gave them the land, that they are "returning" to the land of their ancestors, and that they have a divine right to the land. This particular narrative should not be seen as singular to Israel but as a common pattern used by empires time and time again. Similar theologies were developed by the whites of South Africa to justify apartheid, by the first colonists to ethnically cleanse the Native American population in North America, and by Australians against the Aboriginals.[14] No serious Christian scholar today buys into any of the colonial theologies regarding South Africa or Australia. On the contrary, more churches started asking for forgiveness for siding with colonial powers over and against the native peoples of those countries.

Western and increasingly Asian theologians still ascribe, however, to the myth of a Judeo-Christian tradition. This myth of the Judeo-Christian tradition is unequivocally part of imperial theology that sees and believes itself as supreme. It is utilized theologically and implicitly against the Palestinian people and within the context of the clash of civilization against Islam. The other aspect of imperial theology has to do with the *theologia gloriae* of the so-called Christian Right, with its belief in the role of the State of Israel in the history of salvation and in preparation for the Second Coming of Christ. It is noteworthy that, on the issue of Palestine, both supposedly liberal Western theology and conservative and fundamentalist theology are uncritical of the State of Israel and contain a pro-Israeli bias, choosing to ignore the presence and suffering of the native Palestinian people.

We are still far away from the moment where Western and Jewish theologians will ask Palestinians for forgiveness for the harm done to them and their land in the name of the Divine.

6

The People of Palestine

Often when I meet foreigners, especially from the Global South, and they hear that I'm from the Holy Land, I sense how moved they are. When they learn that I'm from Bethlehem and was born just across the street from where tradition says Jesus was born they often say something like, "Wow, we envy you." But the truth is that living in the land called *Holy* is not to be envied. It is not easy to live in Palestine and survive physically and even more, psychologically and emotionally. It is a distinct and unique challenge to be placed in a buffer zone and often war zone. It is tough to see one's country a battlefield, to see it divided and torn apart. It is enervating to feel that one's country and people are occupied not by an equal but by an empire, albeit by proxy. But this is the context in which the people of Palestine have repeatedly found themselves. This is the context in which the Bible was written. And it is the context Palestinians face today.

This situation generated and continues to generate four existential questions that the people of the land must consciously and continually ask.

WHERE ARE YOU, GOD?

When I cross the checkpoint from Bethlehem to Jerusalem, which looks more like a big prison with watchtowers, trip wires, cameras, turnstiles, metal detectors, and scanning machines, I frequently think that the checkpoint with all its sophisticated surveillance equipment is the manifestation of the empire controlling the flow of goods and peoples and subjugating them. More often than not there are long lines of weary folk waiting to walk through the checkpoint.[1] And only one line out of three existing lines is ever operational. The other two are "out of order." Behind a bullet-proof window sits a young Israeli soldier, not even twenty-five years old, with a machine gun. Outside, people wait in lines for a long time, sometimes hours, while inside things crawl. In the lines are children trying to attend school; nurses who are late for their shifts; old people wishing to go to pray in Jerusalem (after obtaining a permit for one day, if they are fortunate); those seeking medical treatment (if they have permission and the economic means to be treated outside the West Bank); and others. In midsummer it is very hot, smelly, and crowded. People slowly lose patience. They push left and right. Yet nothing moves. The young soldier may be in a bad mood or be texting his girlfriend. And then, suddenly in that cavernous hall, there arises the cry of an old Palestinian woman standing in her hand-embroidered dress, raising both hands toward the sky and imploring loudly in Arabic, "Wenak ya Allah?" meaning "Where are you, God?"

"Where are you, God?" is a three-thousand-year-old lament that the inhabitants of Palestine have passed from one generation to the next. It is a question that echoes throughout the Bible. It is a question of a people whose faith is continually tested. They do not question the existence of God, or his care, but they wonder why God is not moving. He sees his people being oppressed, he knows how they are being treated, and yet he seems to be so silent. The cry is supposed to shake him so that he awakes, acts, and delivers.

Living in a buffer zone and war zone, seeing that which people work so hard to build and call home repeatedly destroyed, being suffocated by the empire, which is intent on being omnipresent and exercising its might, generates this old yet ever-new query, "God, where are you?"

Yet throughout the Bible, with the exception of the Exodus, the God in whom the people of Palestine put their faith appears to be silent. He sees the Assyrians resettling his people and does nothing. He watches the Babylonians desecrate his temple, and he doesn't move an inch. His capital is destroyed by the Romans, and he appears not to care. Even when his only beloved son is hung on the cross, he is *absconditus* and hides (Mk 15:34).

This has been the experience of the people of Palestine throughout history, irrespective of their religious affiliation. When the Persians in 614 destroyed over three thousand churches in Palestine and little was left with the exception of the Church of the Nativity, God did nothing to push the invaders back. When the Crusaders plundered churches in the Holy Land, God did not move a finger. And when the Church of the Nativity was besieged in 2002, neither God nor the so-called Christian world did anything.[2]

The God in which the people of Palestine put their faith seems to be weak and not up to the challenge of the empire. Like his people he does not appear to have the means or resources to confront the empire. He is poor, like his people, which is evident even in the architecture of Palestine. There are no monuments to commemorate his divinity, such as the pyramids in Egypt, or decorated shrines in Mesopotamia, or beautiful buildings still visible in Iran, Turkey, and Rome. And even when he has a dwelling, and although it is built by the sweat of his own poor people, most of the time such a place is constructed not so much for his name but to underline the glory of the empire. The Second Temple was built by a Persian decree and with Persian money (Ezr 1:2), the third by Roman consensus, the Dome of the Rock commissioned by an Arab caliph residing in Syria, and most of the churches of the Holy Land visited by pilgrims in the twenty-first century were built by the Byzantine Empire, Crusaders, or by nineteenth-century European powers. And so the old question still echoes today: "Where are you, God?"

WHO IS MY NEIGHBOR?

The fact that Palestine was often controlled by different empires simultaneously and that it was often divided between north and south, or between the sea versus mountain culture, which was different from the culture of the desert, meant that the people of the land developed diverse and often contrary identities and subcultures. The unity of the land was threatened not solely by various empires but by the divisions of the people inhabiting the land. In such a context it is all too easy for a neighbor to become an enemy and for a fellow countryman or countrywoman to become a stranger.

In many theological writings, especially in the Old Testament or in Jewish studies, there is a tendency to talk about a triangle of God, land, and people. This closely resembles a religious nationalism discourse. A glance at Palestine and its history reveals that there is often more than one "people" inhabiting the land and multiple identities coexisting side by side developing adversarial identities. Yet little attention if any has been given to studying this biblical phenomenon.

I argue that "who is my neighbor?" is the second question found throughout the Bible and up to the modern history of Palestine. The Bible, from Genesis 4 to Revelation 21 can be seen as a collection of narratives on land, peoples, and identities.

The story of Cain and Abel (Gn 4:1–16) is a tale of two prototypes representing the Cenites in the Hebron area in relation to the Jerusalem monarchy. The story of the flood, later in Genesis, concludes with Noah's three sons—Shem, Ham, and Japheth (Gn 10:2–32)—representing three groups of peoples with distinct identities. Babel is the attempt to reverse this diversity and to pervert those orders into a uniformity of one people with one culture, an empire project that ended with confusion (Gn 11:1–9). In the stories of the patriarchs there is a continuing process of election and rejection projecting different notions of relationships among the peoples in the land. Three different traditions from three regions (Abraham in the Negev, Isaac in Beer Sheva, and Jacob in Bethel and Samaria) are unified in a single story of three generations, while a process of selection is undertaken distinguishing Isaac from Ishmael, Jacob from Esau, and Joseph from his brothers, each representing a distinct group. The Exodus story is about a people liberated and led to enter the Promised Land only to find other groups already living there. Joshua and Judges deal with the relations of this group of people to the other peoples of the land. Ruth is about the relationship of that group of people to their neighbors in Jordan, the Moabites. The books of Samuel deal with the desire to have a state, such as their neighbors have, relating a success story of David unifying the whole land with its diverse peoples and Solomon expanding those boundaries to include more peoples (a unification that did not last longer than forty years), which also divided the south and the north similar to the situation before David). Ezra, Nehemiah, and Esther tell the story of returning to the land after the Exile and the new relationship to those who stayed in the land. The prophets speak words of truth to the kings so that they care for the marginalized.

It might be easy to read the Old Testament as a collection of narratives on land, peoples, and identity, but what of the

New Testament? There has, to date, not been much research on this subject. I argue that the whole New Testament is a collection of narratives that challenge the then-existing exclusive national and religious narratives. The New Testament introduces a new lens; instead of identifying with one people over against the others, which is the traditional way of forming one's identity, it calls people to reflect on the entire process of identification as misleading. In the first chapter of the New Testament three non-Israelites are included in Jesus' genealogy (Mt 1:5–6). When northern Palestine was occupied for more than a hundred and fifty years by the Assyrians, its relationship to Judea was tense, and as a result, a full-blown system of apartheid developed. Jesus thus answered the question "Who is my neighbor?" with the parable of the Good Samaritan. It is no surprise that the narratives of the Samaritans are widely included (Lk 10:25–37; 17:11–19; Jn 4:1–42). It is also not coincidental that marginalized sinners and tax collectors are included creating an inclusive community based on social justice (Mt 10:3; 11:19; 21:31; Lk 5:27; 15:1; 18:10; 19:2). Jesus was concerned about reconciling the different groups in the land, knowing that it was a prerequisite to peace when he said:

> Jerusalem, Jerusalem, the city that kills the prophets and stones those who are sent to it! How often have I desired to gather your children together as a hen gathers her brood under her wings, and you were not willing! See, your house is left to you, desolate." (Mt 23:37–38)

It's not by chance that the three Synoptic Gospels end with a call to cross boundaries and reach out into the world, a program beginning "in Jerusalem, in all Judea and Samaria, and to the ends of the earth" (Acts 1:8).

In the Pauline letters the main issue is the gospel of Jesus Christ and its implication for the relationship of the Jews and Gentiles. The letters result from an identity crisis of a Jew from the diaspora, who came to be grounded in Christ, who breached the wall of hostility and created a new inclusive community, a place where "there is no longer Jew or Greek, there is no longer slave or free, there is no longer male or female" (Gal 3:28). The New Testament then concludes with the vision of a new heaven and new earth with a new community formed from all nations and tribes (Rv 5:9).

I am often asked why the Palestinians can't unite. Why can't Fateh and Hamas seem to agree? The answer is related to geopolitics. The two main Palestinian parties do not operate in a vacuum. Regional powers and international politics pull each of them in a different direction. The siege that Israel imposes on Gaza aims at developing two diverse and unrelated identities, one in the West Bank, the other in the Gaza Strip. The stronger these identities develop in isolation from one another, the less likely it is for their people to unite. "Who is my neighbor?" becomes an extremely critical and personal question. There are stories about brothers from the same family. One joins Fateh while the other joins Hamas, and suddenly they stop talking to each other and become bitter enemies. It is ironic that world leaders today constantly urge the Palestinians to "talk" to the Israelis, while they advise them pointedly not to talk to each other, meaning Fateh and Hamas.

THE WAY TO LIBERATION?

When I studied in Germany in the 1980s, I went to a gathering of Palestinian students one evening. There was a lively discussion taking place, with the students debating the best way to liberate Palestine from the Israeli occupation. Each faction within the student union had a fixed idea about how freedom would be achieved. Some were calling for negotiations as the means to a permanent and just peace; others insisted, "What is taken by force, can only be restored by force." Some said that the road to liberation is only possible through Arab unity, and there was one lonely student who espoused, "Islam is the only solution." In the 1980s there was still a very active Palestinian Liberation Organization, and Hamas had not yet been created. I have to admit that for me, at that time, the way to liberate Palestine was by finishing my doctoral dissertation and returning to serve my people through the church.

The fact that the people of Palestine have largely been under occupation by regional powers and empires throughout their history begs the crucial and existential question, What is the best way to obtain liberation? Although occupation has been the rule in Palestine, most people never absorbed the fact that occupation was a reality with which they had to learn to live; rather, they saw it as the exception that had to end. And yet there was no consensus among the people of Palestine on how best to achieve liberation. There were always different responses about how to end the occupation. In studying the different answers given to this question throughout history, five different models or phenomena are easily identifiable. I take the context of the New Testament with which Christians are most familiar to show these threads. Interestingly, these five threads or patterns are still visible and prominent in Palestine today.

Fighting Back

Fighters are not a permanent phenomenon in Palestine but rather are the exception in Palestine's history.[3] Most of the time life in Palestine appears to be "business as usual." To both outsiders and insiders, it might seem the people of Palestine have surrendered to the empire. But this impression has always proved to be deceitful. Suddenly, the situation would grow out of control. The catalyst that would lead to organized resistance would come as a result of any of a number of different factors: excessive use of brutal force by the occupiers, increased taxation, or religious insult, among others. It was all just too much.

The usual reaction of the people of Palestine has been a type of popular protest: demonstrations, throwing stones at the occupiers, or attacking a soldier. The response of the empire has for the most part been uniform: military mobilization, invasion, and even greater force. Whenever something like this happened, it was a sure indication that a revolt or Intifada was on its way. In the course of a revolt or Intifada zealous fighters start to appear, who believe they have to respond and fight back, thinking that they can teach the occupiers a lesson. So they would organize a plan and engage in military operations against the occupiers and their troops. For them, the sword was a kind of guerrilla operation; it was the best and only way to liberation. They were ready to fight and even die for their country and its liberation.

> Ironic as it may seem, Roman practices produced the very groups that continued and prolonged the war. That is, the methods used by the Roman forces in reconquering Jewish Palestine created the conditions which gave rise to epidemic banditry and escalating peasant revolt, precisely what they were trying to suppress.[4]

Such groups have appeared in almost every Intifada in ancient and in modern times. The average lifespan of an Intifada is three to five years.[5] That seems to be the length of time or capacity of the people of Palestine for enduring direct military confrontation. The longer an Intifada continues, the more it becomes a liability for the population. Often the motivation of these people is not based solely on a strong sense of nationalism but also on religion. Such freedom fighters emerged during the Second Intifada (2000–2004) in Palestine.[6] Their pictures, with machine guns in hand (bought from the Israelis), were televised globally.

Strangely enough, if one visits the Herodion, a fortress built by Herod the Great in the first century BC, near Bethlehem, where many fighters retreated during the Jewish revolts against the Romans, one can see several plaques hung by Israeli settlers commemorating the heroic acts of those first-century fighters. They are held in high esteem as Jewish freedom fighters against the Roman Empire. And yet, Palestinian fighters who stand in the same tradition are labeled by the Israelis as terrorists. Either groups from the first century and those from the twenty-first century both should be considered freedom fighters or both considered terrorists. And yet two groups with similar ideologies are viewed with vastly different standards. As mentioned before, it is also important to realize that *terrorist* is a description coined by the empire for those fighting the empire with the weapons of the empire. For the occupied, those fighting are regarded as *freedom fighters.*

Revolt against the harshness of occupation and empire was never the response of the majority in Palestine but only of a tiny minority. And it was never universally endorsed, even by people of the land themselves. In studying the history of Palestine over the centuries it is clear that none of the Intifadas or revolts brought liberation, except that of the Maccabees from 164 BC to 160 BC. All other revolts were brutally crushed.

Observing the Law

While fighters were mainly a marginal phenomenon in terms of the numbers of people involved, the most popular answer to liberation was that given in the New Testament by the Pharisees.[7] These were a group of laypeople who didn't believe that the response to the occupation was political but argued that it was religious; that is, the empire was nothing but a punishment brought by God because the people of the land had forgotten his law. For them, the empire was the manifestation of heathenism. And heathenism could be pushed back only if the law of God became the norm of life for all of his people. The defeat of heathenism would bring about the defeat of the empire. To that end the Pharisees were busy spreading the law, creating additional laws, and competing to fulfill every iota of the law's tenets.

Unfortunately, the Pharisees have been misrepresented in much of Christian theology, becoming the prototype of religious hypocrites. Although the Pharisees were concerned with orthodoxy and gave a great deal of authority to tradition, they were also surprisingly highly pragmatic. "The Torah could be so interpreted as to contain what the teachers read into it, but nothing of which they could not approve. And the Traditions of the fathers, insofar as they contained Divine truths, had to agree with the ever-growing and ever-unfolding conscience of the people."[8] The way in which post-Holocaust theology has tried to portray the Pharisees is also problematic. Both approaches fail to help us understand what the Pharisees really wanted. I remember being in a theological consultation in Bern, Switzerland, some years ago and hearing a French-speaking theologian praise the way the Pharisees understood the law and what it really meant if rightly understood. Listening to this theological post-Holocaust nostalgia, I couldn't remain quiet. After the man finished, I raised my hand and said, "Let me put what you have just said in political terminology. What you have just presented is very much the political manifesto of Hamas [Islamic Resistance Movement]."

He was shocked. The last thing he had in mind was to equate the Pharisees with Hamas, whom he could not relate to positively.

I said, "The group who is promoting the law today as the solution to the Palestinian problem is Hamas. The Arabic word for law is *sharia*. For Hamas, as part of the Muslim Brotherhood movement, *sharia* is the way to true liberation. The fact that Hamas has been engaged in fighting Israel since 1988 should not make us think that this group belongs to the zealots. On the contrary, in all Muslim Brotherhood writings, the main focus is on having divine law control peoples' daily lives. Their main fight is not with the empire, but with their own people who have forgotten their religious identity."

The political program of the Islamic Brotherhood, until the outbreak of the so-called Arab Spring, was to Islamize society slowly but surely; to ensure that all adhere to religion. This is the true liberation.

This particular response to religion is highly attractive to an occupied people because it can produce concrete results. It is difficult to show results by fighting the empire, but a marked increase in the number of people adhering to the law is always impressive. The numbers of veiled women, the number of men with beards, the number of people going to prayers are all quantifiable. And it is an appealing and human response to people who feel crushed by the empire, whose dignity has been tested, whose rights have been violated, and who, deep down, feel that God might have forgotten about them.

The logic of those following the law is this: "God does not respond because we are not good enough. He forgot us because we have forgotten him. He left us because we left him. But he will return with full might if we return to his law, the *sharia*."

Because they are pragmatic, they do not hesitate to assume power if the context is ripe. The Pharisees grabbed power after the destruction of the temple in AD 70, just as the Muslim Brotherhood is attempting to fill the power vacuum after the collapse of nation states in the twenty-first century. No Western theologian who is impressed by divine laws would wish to live in a place actually governed by them, where all people in the society are told what to eat and what not to drink; where women are assigned certain dress codes and seats so as not to come close to men; and where religious laws are forced on people so as to leave them no option to make their own decisions.

Accommodation

A totally different answer at the time of Jesus was given by the Sadducees. These Jews, serving in connection with the Temple, had a religious function, although the service in the Temple since Persian times was under imperial supervision. This group was, therefore, somehow connected to both the people and the empire that was in power. The Sadducees were a small but influential group, well connected and aristocratic. Their influence derived from the fact that they understood the dynamics of the street and those in power. They were also a pragmatic sort but in a unique way. Their slogan could have been: We don't like the empire, but as long as it is here, we have to deal with it. The question for them was not one of liberation but of transitional accommodation. They always walked a tightrope. The most important issue for them was: What is God's, and what is the emperor's? (see Lk 20:20–26). They had to ensure that they pleased both the people and those in power. The influence of this group stemmed from the fact that its members often played the role of mediator between the people and the empire. They brought the issues of the people before those in power, and they also transmitted the wishes of the empire to the occupied. Their power derived from being in charge of the Temple and its religious ceremonies. This pattern is typical for people living in the shadow of the empire who must continuously seek accommodation. Some would see the religious and aristocratic leaders, as well as certain members of the political and religious leadership in Palestine, as belonging to this category, because they represent the people, yet their "authority" often has to be confirmed and approved by the occupying power.

Collaboration

The fourth group has yet another point of view. Their slogan could be: If you can't beat them, join them. These were and are the people who are opportunists, who seek to benefit from the empire by doing business with it. They were the tax collectors in Jesus' day, whose income depended solely on the sums of money collected from their fellow countrymen and the percentage they kept for themselves. No empire can survive without these people.

In today's Palestine these are the subcontractors who distribute Israeli products to the Palestinian markets, who bid on subcontracts in Israeli settlements, or who collaborate by providing information on people and organizations. This group wants to exploit the empire by helping to exploit its own people. For this group, the empire is good for business. Why fight for liberation? Long live the empire!

Retrieval

A fifth answer was given by the community of Qumran.[9] Its people were disillusioned and disappointed by their religious leadership, which they viewed as compromising too much with the empire. This group was also frightened by the invading culture of the empire, which led to a drastic change in the behavior of the people of Palestine. The Qumranites had the feeling that the world was lost, corrupt, and evil. The only possible response, therefore, was to retreat from the world into the desert and into small communities where they could create an alternative social structure. This structure would enable the people to adhere to and uphold the old rules and concentrate on the pure teachings of the law in anticipation and preparation for the final battle against the evil empire.

This group is still around. They are the Muslim Salafists and some of the conservative Christian free churches that are disappointed by their religious leadership and shocked by the rapid Westernization of their society. So they retreat. They lose hope in any change, forming small groups of followers who band together, come what may, studying, praying, and eating as a community. The followers of these groups are usually poor and consequently marginalized. Retreating to a basic dress code and a simpler lifestyle is a real relief for them. They don't need to keep up with an increasingly consumer-oriented society. Being disillusioned and disinterested in politics, they maintain a faithful watch preparing for the great battle against the evil of the present.

These are just five patterns in the New Testament whose traces can be found in Palestine today. These patterns are neither rigid nor always visible. The context is never static; the situation is as fluid as history is dynamic. But somehow the above-mentioned themes keep emerging. Additionally, there are also hybrid models. Sometimes people shift from one group to another. Many don't belong to any of these groups. There are other modern answers to the question of liberation. Many believe in education as the best means for liberation; others believe in building a strong economy and investing in Palestine as a way to liberate the economy from the occupier's fist. Others have given up hope and can't see liberation within sight. They don't want their children to go through what they have faced, so they migrate to the "Promised Land" of the West in order to find jobs, stability, and freedom.

WHEN WILL WE HAVE A STATE?

Because Palestine has been almost continuously occupied during its history, the fourth important question raised repeatedly is: When are we going to have our own state? People look at the gargantuan dimensions of the empire and hope for a mini-state. Liberation is not an end to itself. The end game for them must be a state. The people of Palestine have often looked around and seen functioning states, some of them mightier than others, and then recognized, to their dismay, that they lack one. Their desire was and is simply to be "like other nations" (1 Sm 8:20). They imagine that having a state is the solution to facing up to the empire. A state will protect them, take care of them, and provide the necessary infrastructure for them to survive.

This was the question put by the elders of Israel to the prophet Samuel, but it is also found in the New Testament. It is thought provoking to read that after the resurrection of Christ, when he appeared to his disciples on the Mount of Olives in Jerusalem, the first and only query the disciples could come up with was, "Lord, is this the time when you will restore the kingdom to Israel?" (Acts 1:6). The issue about the timing of a state is omnipresent in Palestine. The fact that this question was still on the minds of the disciples after everything that had happened during passion week and after the stone was rolled away from the tomb shows how important it was in the minds of the people of Palestine then. Indeed, it is still so today. The necessity of Palestinian statehood has in the last few years been close to the top of the world agenda. The Palestinians have gone to the United Nations saying the time has come, and it is indeed long overdue, for the recognition of Palestine as a state among the 193 nation states of the world.[10] The fact that global state recognition can be achieved only with the blessing of the empire is an indication of what a Palestinian state in the future could or would be able to do.

After the disciples had listened to Jesus' teaching for three years, they still seemed fixated on the question, "Lord, is this the time when you will restore the kingdom to Israel?" Interestingly, if one reads the Bible, it is highly realistic about what a state in Palestine could and would do. The state is seen somehow as a logical necessity—but not as the solution. In fact, the Bible is critical about most of the Israelite kings whose failure, in biblical language, is that they "sinned against the Lord. . . . They followed other gods" (2 Kgs 17:7). In political words, one might say they had a state and a king but still couldn't be independent because even those kings were inferior to the empire and were dependent on it. In fact, the people of Palestine would often look skeptically, if not satirically, at their kings, as some looked at Saul, saying, "How can this man save us?" (1 Sm 10:27). There is much truth to this, because rulers in Palestine were mostly part of the empire, and as such the people of Palestine did not adopt and develop a positive attitude toward their own kings and rulers. This was far different than in the empires where a pharaoh or emperor had almost divine status.

Comparing the attitude of Palestinians today to the Palestinian Authority and the standing that Assad once had in Syria or Mubarak in Egypt, it is easy to see how these different attitudes and approaches to rulers have survived up to the present. Geo-politically, the largest area possible for Palestine to have as a state is a joke compared with the vast areas empires once occupied and are occupying. A state might thus be important, but statehood would not change much in terms of geo-politics and power balance. This is why the states that emerged in Palestine over the centuries resembled little more than areas of self-rule in the shadow of the empire. Today, in a post-national era and in the era of the global marketplace dominated by multinational corporations, the question of small states is even more pressing. If Israelis and Palestinians are frank with themselves, they need to admit that the state project they respectively worked so hard to achieve for the last sixty or so years has failed. Israel developed an apartheid system, and the Palestinian mini-state in Gaza or the Palestinian "holes in the cheese" of the West Bank are not the dream for which people fought. Yet, both peoples are still unable and/ or unwilling to admit that hard and painful truth and begin looking for new models of coexistence.

7

God

The presence of an all-powerful empire provoked the cry, "Where are you, God?" But this doesn't mean that God was absent from the equation. On the contrary, the question aims at truly inviting him into the equation because in the face of an omnipotent empire the occupied have no one to turn to but God. When people are overwhelmed by the power of empire and drowning in the feeling that no other state or people can help them defeat the empire, there is no option about where to seek help. When they lose faith in changing the geo-political balance sheet by human means, God alone remains. This was and is not the case only in ancient Palestine. Much of the religious fundamentalism in the Middle East today has to do with an overwhelming sense of disempowerment in the face of an imperial power. When, because of the veto of the empire, the appeal to human conscience and basic human rights fails to assist in bringing justice to the oppressed, there is no choice and no one to seek help from but God. Is God, therefore, just a scapegoat? Does he merely fill a void? Is he merely an illusion?

The answer is, none of the above. Believing that there is something more powerful than the empire is an important and necessary step toward questioning it. God questions the omnipotence of the empire. As well, seeing God on the other side of the empire queries and challenges the morality of the empire, which is a key link in its weakening. Faith in God becomes a strong factor in mobilizing people against the empire. Whereas armies might not dare to challenge the empire because of the power imbalance, faith in God can provide the necessary motivation to go against the empire even if doing so means sacrificing one's life. The empire thus provokes God and God becomes a factor in dismantling the empire. Phenomenologically, this has been seen repeatedly throughout history.

The three monotheistic religions did not take root in and grow out of the Middle East haphazardly. And it is not coincidental that the Bible emerged from Palestine, not from one of the empires. It is, in fact, this context of ongoing oppression, of forever living in the shadow of the empire, that brought about the birth of both Judaism and Christianity, and across the sea, Islam.

REVELATION

The existence of God, according to the Bible, is not the chief content of revelation. God is worshiped in numerous countries and cultures. Ancient empires also had their own impressive gods. It wasn't the notion that there *is* a God that was revelatory, but the response to that existential question, "Where are you, God?" The people of Palestine were able to discover a unique answer to this question, and the answer made history.

God was visible and omnipresent in the empire with shrines and temples that represented not only his glory but also that of the empire. God's omnipotence and that of the empire were almost interchangeable. He was a victorious God, a fitting deity for a victorious empire.

At the other end of the spectrum there was the God of the people of Palestine, whose tiny territory resembled a corridor in Middle Eastern geography. His country lacked resources. Palestine boasts no Nile or Euphrates. Without water its people have always been dependent on rainfall for their needs. This God had to see his people repeatedly endure starvation and migrate to neighboring countries for food and supplies. Above all, this God appeared to be weak compared with other gods. He seemed forever to be on the losing end, just like his people. This God was almost interchangeable with his people, his weakness was shown in theirs, and their defeat was his. This God was a loser. He lost almost all wars, and his people were forced to pay the price of those defeats. In short, this God did not appear to be up to the challenge of the various empires. His people in Palestine were forced to hear the mocking voices of their neighbors who taunted them, "Where is your God?" (Ps 42: 3, 10).

• The revelation the people of Palestine received was the ability to spot God where no one else was able to see him. When his people were driven as slaves into Babylon, they witnessed him accompanying them. When his capital, Jerusalem, was destroyed and his temple plundered, they saw him there. When his people were defeated, he was also present. The salient feature of this God was that he didn't run away when his people faced their destiny but remained with them, showing solidarity and choosing to share their destiny. Consequently and ultimately, Jesus revealed this God on the cross, in a situation of terrible agony and pain, when he was brutally crushed by the empire and hung like a rebellious freedom fighter. The people of Palestine could then say with great certainty: "For we do not have a high priest who is unable to sympathize with our weaknesses, but we have one who in every respect has been tested as we are" (Heb 4:15).

⚑ For the people of Palestine this meant that defeat in the face of the empire was not an ultimate defeat.[1] It meant that after the country was devastated by the Babylonians, when everything seemed to be lost, a new beginning was possible. Even when the dwelling place of God was destroyed, God survived that destruction, developing in response a dwelling that was indestructible. And when Jesus cried on the cross, "My God, my God, why have you forsaken me?" (Mk 15:34), that soul-rending plea was just the prelude to the resurrection. The revelation made in Palestine was that God was to be found where no one expected him. To Gentiles this sounded like "foolishness," and for Jews it was a "stumbling block," but for Paul such a revelation was nothing less than "the power of God and the wisdom of God" (1 Cor 1:23–24).

Is this simply a nice homiletical interpretation? No! This revelation was and is of utmost importance geo-politically. For it enabled the people of Palestine to survive all defeats. It made the defeat lose its teeth, death lose its sting, and empire lose its victory (see 1 Cor 15:55). It ensured that empires were incapable of celebrating their victories, because while they crushed the people they occupied, they weren't able to crush their spirit. ●

As a pastor, when I counsel engaged couples, one issue I try to address is how to deal with marriage problems. Problems are normal in marriages. But a couple needs to learn that issues should not become "the problem," but rather that problems are there to solve and cope with; they are not the end of a marriage but a phase from which the couple should emerge stronger. This is precisely what the aforementioned revelation did for the people of Palestine. It helped them not to surrender after each defeat but to pick themselves up and start over again. It made them develop an art of surviving extremist empires, "afflicted in every way, but not crushed; perplexed, but not driven to despair; persecuted, but not forsaken; struck down, but not destroyed" (2 Cor 4:8–9).

The art of survival and starting anew is a highly developed form of expression in Palestine, and one I see daily. People's lives, businesses, and education are interrupted by wars and the aftermath of wars over and over again, and yet I witness people refusing to give up, taking a deep breath, and beginning again. Logically, it is foolish, and yet there is deep wisdom in such a course of action. I'm often asked by visitors how I can keep going. Everything seems to be lost, the land "settled" by Israel, the wall suffocating Palestinian land and spirit, the world silent, and hope almost gone. The answer to that is not psychological but theological: There is no way to understand and face the status quo but at the logic of God.

GOD AS A FACTOR IN GEO-POLITICS

There is another side to the question. Does this theology have geo-political relevance, or is it just a matter of psychology? Does it change anything on the ground, or is it just a way of helping people cope with the situation? Is God of any relevance to the geo-politics of the Middle East? Has he become a factor in the equation? This is a critical issue that I have yet to hear discussed. People begin with geo-political realities and conclude with theologies. My thesis is that God came to defeat geo-politics and he succeeded. Because without God, Palestine would have continued as a land at the periphery. Yet because God chose to reveal himself in this land, it became central to history, which is why it is found at the center of ancient maps. Because of God. The moment God identified himself with this land, everything changed. Who would have heard of the Jordan River if it were not part of the salvation history? Compared with the rivers of the empires, the Jordan is not even a creek. The day that Jesus was baptized in that river, it became more famous than the Nile, the Euphrates, and the Tigris combined.

Who would have heard of my hometown, the little town called Bethlehem, situated on the top of a hill with no geo-political importance? However, the moment this city was seen as the place of the incarnation of God, though "one of the little clans of Judah" (Mi 5:2), it was declared to be "by no means least among the rulers of Judah" (Mt 2:6). I'm amazed and humbled when I visit churches in other parts of the world. If possible, in addition to preaching, I like to give the children's sermon. I love it when children are gathered in the front of the sanctuary, and we sit on the steps leading to the altar and talk. They are usually small children who have not yet entered first grade. Often they do not even know the name of their own city or community. But when I ask them if they know where Jesus was born, they immediately reply, "Bethlehem!" I'm always impressed. Wherever I am, in China or the United States, Germany or South Africa, children know the name of my birthplace before they are aware of the name of their own birthplace. This was made possible by God.

And who would ever have had the desire to visit that town called Jerusalem if it were not for God? The moment God chose Jerusalem as the place for his throne, people began flocking to Jerusalem. Without God, Jerusalem would have been left in ruins like so many other destroyed towns in Palestine and throughout the Middle East. But because of his revelation, all empires competed to build something there. Even today, without the religious establishments in Jerusalem, there would be little of significance—no synagogues, churches, or mosques; no schools and hospitals; no consulates or headquarters of international organizations; no businesses, hotels, or travel agencies. Without God, Jerusalem would be one of the most boring places on earth.

As well, without God, Palestine would receive no media attention whatsoever. The political situation in Palestine is often tense, and thus media coverage is deserved. But there are scores of other conflict zones globally where the situation is far worse, where famine, wars, and destruction are terribly severe, and yet those places fail to make headlines. If it were not for the good news that came out of Palestine two thousand years ago, Palestine would not be newsworthy. I was once told that the number of journalists in Jerusalem is second worldwide only to Washington. I'm not sure if this is still true, but the point is that without the history of salvation, Palestine, with its geo-political standing, would receive no attention whatsoever. The land on the periphery became the focus of the world's attention because and only because of God.

God came to Palestine to change the dynamics of the geo-political reality, and he succeeded. Without him, Palestine would have been a mere battlefield, and the most hopeless place on earth. But because of the Divine, the battlefield became holy ground. I often encounter the assumption that Palestine is a battleground because it is the Holy Land, and empires want to control it. There is some truth to this. But the opposite is even more true. Palestine without God would have been but a corridor for invading armies and the most suitable and logical spot for regional battles. This country needed God badly to transform the battlefield into holy land. For the people of Palestine this was and is highly significant. Who wants to live on a battlefield? Who can survive such a context? What sense would it make to continue to live in such a place? It's only because God chose this land as the place for his revelation that this otherwise bloody land became holy. Palestine is not fought over because it is holy; but it became holy to change its status and to be upgraded from a battle-field to holy ground. If God had not chosen this land, life in it would be totally unbearable; no one would be here except thieves and wolves. But because it was made sacred, people discern a calling in remaining here. They are willing to bear the unbearable, and they are capable of putting up with all the unholy wars of humankind because this is the land of the heavenly King.

Another false assumption I hear ad infinitum from secular-ists is that most of the problems in the Middle East are con-nected to religion. Secularists see religion as one of the main reasons for the seemingly intractable problems in the region.

They think that getting rid of religion is the grand solution to the conflict. They then point to all the forms of fundamentalism connected to the three monotheistic religions. But this is not quite the case. It is true that religion is often part of the problem rather than being part of the solution. And I like to say that in the Middle East we have too much religion, and that less would definitely be more in this arena. But I also say that we have too much in the way of politics. The current wave of fundamentalism in the Middle East would not exist if politicians were successful in their work. The politics of the superpowers in the last two centuries and the failure of international governing bodies in creating a just peace have pushed people to religion. When politicians fail the hopes of people, who can blame them for seeking help in God? And when empires get drunk on their own power and behave like deities, people feel they must challenge such a mindset with God's might on their side. When human institutions, which were created to safeguard peace, fail to bring freedom to people enduring one of the longest continuous occupations in modern history, God has to step up demanding, "Let my people go!" (Ex 8:1).

8

Jesus

In an essay entitled "Jesus and Empire," Richard A. Horsley writes:

> From the perspective of the past several years in the early twenty-first century it may seem remarkable to us now that the "historic Jesus" of the twentieth century managed to remain remarkably apolitical throughout a century of unprecedented political turmoil. Neither the holocaust of six million Jews nor decades of anticolonial revolts and their suppression by the European colonial powers led to a broad questioning of standard assumptions, perspective, and approach. Only after the United States blatantly asserted its "hard" power in the Middle East, in the invasion and occupation of Iraq, did more than a handful of biblical interpreters begin to question the received wisdom.[1]

I couldn't agree more, but I would also note that after almost half a century of Israeli occupation of Palestinian land, Western theologians have been unable to see that the empire is at work in Israel itself. The conventional wisdom about the Jewish state is still not probed even by the most articulate postcolonial biblical interpreters. It is past time, therefore, to reinterpret the words of Jesus and to ensure that his wisdom regarding the empire applies to the state of Israel as a modern expression of the empire, albeit by proxy, and discover its relevance to the Middle East today.

What responses did Jesus proclaim in the face of the empire? What was his philosophy toward liberating his people? How did his way differ from the other answers of his time, and what did he teach to that end? Is there anything new that Jesus brought to the table regarding the way in which faith ought to face the empire? The topic of Jesus and the empire has experienced a revival in the last ten years, and there is ample research on how the different authors of the New Testament viewed empire. In this chapter I show how Jesus' way is seen in the context of Palestine.

THE MESSIAH IS HERE!

When facing a powerful and cruel empire, oppressed people often grow so overwhelmed that they give up hope of any conceivable human change. The only hope that remains on the horizon is the Messiah. There appears to be no solution attainable by political or religious means. The empire is so powerful that only direct divine intervention by an anointed savior, the Messiah, can bring about desired change. This earthly world is so corrupted by power that it requires a higher being to deal with it. And as is so often the case in the context of permanent conflict and oppression, the only one who can challenge the emperor is the Messiah. Oppressed people wait for the Messiah because they realize that God will not tolerate the empire forever. God will respond in his time, and people must accordingly wait patiently in full anticipation of his coming.

The traces of this anticipation are found throughout the Old and New Testaments. The early Christians saw the promised Messiah in Jesus. Other Jewish groups couldn't see this. But waiting for a Messiah wasn't just a phenomenon of the first century. Indeed, it is so deeply entrenched in Middle Eastern thinking that it is still found today in many forms. Anti-Zionist, ultra-Orthodox Jews are clear on this subject. They reject the modern state of Israel because they believe that only the Messiah can declare such a state. All other attempts to do so are doomed to fail. This group of Jews is, therefore, supportive of an independent Palestinian state. They even have a representative in the Palestinian National Council. In discussion with some religious Muslim groups one can often discern the desire for someone such as Saladin, who defeated the Crusaders in the twelfth century and established the Ayyubid dynasty.

The fact that the early Christians saw the Messiah in Jesus brought change to the Middle Eastern scene. The belief that the Messiah had arrived meant divine intervention was not something still to come in the future but was already present. It was here but not fully. While in the early centuries Christian writers were under the impression that the Second Coming of the Messiah and his parousia were at hand, and that the parousia would bring about ultimate change, just a few decades later it became clear that the Second Coming was definitely not approaching rapidly.

With this recognition there came an understanding that the coming of the Messiah in Jesus had itself brought a pivotal change. Christians need no longer wait for direct divine intervention, because the intervention has already take place. The Messiah has come, and there is no need to wait for another. He said what needed to be said and he did what needed to be done. God had done his part. The ball was now in the court of humankind. Either we could choose to play the game or to walk away. Further waiting was a waste of time. The transformed faithful were to engage the world, to challenge the monopoly of power, and to live the life of an already liberated people. This was a remarkable sea-change in the prevailing culture of the Middle East. The belief in Jesus as the yearned-for Messiah replaced the idea of divine intervention with direct intervention of the faithful. It was now those who believed in Christ who had to step into this world to engage and to bring change to the empire.

HISTORY *LONGUE DURÉE*

One of the sentences of Jesus that requires reinterpretation is "Blessed are the meek, for they will inherit the earth" (Mt 5:5). This text is taken from the Sermon on the Mount according to Matthew (Mt 5—7). Compared with the other beatitudes of that sermon, this one is marginalized and seldom receives attention. The phrase "Blessed are the peacemakers" is frequently cited and preached about, but we rarely hear "Blessed are the meek, for they will inherit the earth." Indeed, Luke doesn't even mention this verse but skips it altogether (Lk 6:20–26). Interestingly, Luke likes to talk about the poor, the hungry, and the thirsty, but not about the meek! There is no mention of the meek, perhaps precisely because they are meek. But I think we don't talk about meekness because it's very difficult to spiritualize this verse. "Blessed are the poor in spirit, for theirs is the kingdom of heaven" can be easily spiritualized. Not so with the meek who are to inherit the earth, which refers to something concrete. The verse doesn't say they will inherit the kingdom of God; it says "the earth."

This verse must have been largely ignored initially because it was translated incorrectly. Originally the verse was taken from Psalm 37, in which context the psalm doesn't talk about "the earth"—it talks about "the land." In fact, "the land" is repeated several times in that psalm. Matthew 5:5, therefore, should read, "Blessed are the meek, for they will inherit the Land." That perhaps makes better sense. Psalm 37 doesn't talk about the land near and far; it speaks about a *certain* land,

Palestine. When Jesus said that the meek will inherit the land, everyone at the time knew what was meant by the land. He meant the Holy Land, Palestine. When the words of Jesus were translated from Aramaic into Greek, the word that means "the land" was changed to read "the earth." In fact, in Arabic the word *al-ard* means both "earth" and "land." Translation is interpretation. "Earth" replaced "land."

Such twisting of a biblical text is an old problem and occurs frequently. The Gospels are closely connected to a certain land. For the early church, located outside of Palestine, talking about the earth made far more sense. Why should somebody in Rome worry about who would inherit Palestine? They were concerned about their souls, and maybe about their land, but not about some distant land. Yet, one cannot understand the Gospels if they are disconnected from their original context, which is Palestine. This is why one of the early church fathers claimed that there is a fifth Gospel in addition to the four—the land of Palestine. We cannot understand what the Bible is saying if we don't understand the geography, the geo-politics, and the history of Palestine. But I would argue that there is also something like a sixth Gospel. If we really want to understand the Bible, we need to start listening to it with the ears of the people of the land.

I struggled with this text for many, many years. It simply didn't make sense to me. I don't like to spiritualize things, because I think Jesus was very spiritual precisely because he always spoke to reality, refusing to avoid it, which was the essence of his spirituality. For a long while I thought that Jesus had been mistaken. One needs only to look around the West Bank to realize who controls the land. Sixty percent of the West Bank is controlled by the Israeli army and Jewish settlers. This glaring reality is one of the largest land thefts in modern history, worth hundreds of billions of dollars. If one looks at the Israeli settlements, which ring the West Bank, it is all too obvious that the empire has inherited the land. Listening to the words of Jesus through Palestinian ears, therefore, isn't much help; it doesn't make sense of Jesus' words. Jesus must have been mistaken! It is all too obvious that the military occupation controls the land, and that it also controls that land's resources, including the electromagnetic fields. Everything is controlled by the empire. The empire, not the meek, inherits the land. Jesus was mistaken because the meek are crushed. Their land is being confiscated to make place for people brought in by the empire. Jesus was mistaken.

But in the last five years, while struggling with this text, I have come to read it with new lenses, and the verse now makes sense. In the process I discovered something more powerful than I expected. Matthew 5:5 actually speaks directly to reality in a way I never imagined. It is necessary to use *longue durée* lenses, because if the verse is read with regular lenses, one will never grasp its true meaning. My mistake had been to read history only with the current empire in mind. The prevailing empire took all of my attention. This is the problem if we look at the Israeli-Palestinian conflict only from a perspective of the last sixty years. If we look solely at the last six decades, the word of Jesus doesn't make sense at all. But Jesus had a wide-angle lens, and he looked at history *longue durée*. For the people at Jesus' time, the occupation began with the Romans. Jesus had a far greater understanding of the history of Palestine. He looked at a thousand years all at once, and he saw a chain of empires. There isn't a single regional empire that at some point did not occupy Palestine. The first empire to occupy Palestine was that of the Assyrians, in 722 BC; it stayed for over two hundred years. The Assyrians were replaced by the Babylonians in 587 BC, who didn't last because they were pushed out by the Persians in 538 BC. The Persians didn't stay long either, because they were forced to leave by Alexander the Great. Then there were the Romans. Two thousand years after Jesus we can continue reciting the list of empires that ruled Palestine: the Byzantines, the Arabs, the Crusaders, the Ayyubids, the Ottomans, the British, and last but not least, the Israeli occupation. We have been trained to naively connect Israel today with the Israel of the Bible, instead of connecting it to the above chain of occupying empires. If we focus on the latter, Jesus' words make perfect sense. None of those empires lasted in Palestine forever. They came and stayed for fifty, one hundred, two hundred, a maximum four hundred years, but in the end they were all blown away, gone with the wind.

When occupied people face the empire, they generally become so overwhelmed by its power that they start to think that the empire will remain forever and that it has eternal power. Jesus wanted to tell his people that the empire would not last, that empires come and go. When empires collapse and depart it is the poor and the meek who remain. The "haves" from the people of the land emigrate; they seek to grow richer within the centers of empire. Those who are well educated are "brain drained" and vacuumed up by the empire. Who remains in the land? The meek, that is, the powerless! Empires come and go, while the meek inherit the land. Jesus' wisdom is staggering. It seems to me we have been blinded by a theology that failed to help us understand what Jesus was really saying. Some might disagree, insisting that the Israeli occupation is different. They say: "Look at the settlements. How can you claim they will be gone one day? Look at the wall. How can you say it will be dismantled?" But Israel is no different from the empires of the past. The native people of Palestine, who lived at the time of Jesus and saw the military checkpoints that Herod the Great had created—Herodion, Masada, and many others—would never have imagined that Herod and his empire were not there permanently. If one looks at the "settlements" and cities built by Herod and his sons—Caesarea Maritima, Caesarea Philippi, Sepphoris, Tiberias, Sebastopol, Jerusalem, and many others—and if one lived at the time of Jesus, it would have been almost inconceivable to question the durability of the Roman Empire. Jesus was telling the Palestinian Jews that the Romans who had built those settlements would not be there forever. They would vanish because Palestine would be inherited by the meek. Is this a cheap hope in a distant future? No. Jesus wanted to release the powerless from the power of the empire. The moment he spoke those words, the empire lost its power over the people, and power was transferred to where it rightly belongs, with the people.

FAITH AS RESISTANCE

It wasn't enough for Jesus to know or believe that the empire was not in Palestine to stay. That would have been a passive faith. For Jesus, it was imperative that faith was also active in dismantling the empire. Resistance becomes an act of faith. A fine example of this is given by Matthew in chapter 17. After the transfiguration on the mountain, the disciples were confronted with a boy with a demon. Demons are powers that grab control of people and render them helpless. In that sense they are a perfect symbol for the empire. The disciples were shocked that after being on the top of the mountain, they couldn't heal this boy, and they asked Jesus why. Jesus replied, "Because of your little faith. For truly I tell you, if you have faith the size of a mustard seed, you will say to this mountain, 'Move from here to there,' and it will move; and nothing will be impossible for you" (Mt 17:20–21).

We like to preach about faith that moves mountains. It has almost become a Christian cliché. And yet the text doesn't speak of moving mountains in general but of "this mountain." It is impossible for us to say to which mountain Jesus was referring or pointing. And yet, a single mountain comes to mind if one is familiar with the history and geography of Palestine. One of the wonders of Jesus' time was a mountain that was moved by none other than Herod the Great. In the first century BC, Herod the Great wanted to create a mausoleum for himself. To that end he chose a hill in the Judean desert southeast of Bethlehem and built a castle on top of it. Instead of leaving the castle standing as it was, he ordered it covered outside with earth and soil. People looking at it today do not see a castle but a huge semi-volcanic mountain. This project was the first artificial mountain of its kind in Palestine and must have been the talk of that decade. It was omnipresent. It dominated the Judean desert and hills standing in bold bluntness as a visible testimony to the greatness, power, and vision of Herod and the massive empire and the ego behind him.

Moving this mountain from its place was possible. All that was needed was faith "the size of a mustard seed." This mountain was moved originally thanks to the engineers of the empire and its power, who exploited the poor of Palestine as cheap laborers to build such symbols of the empire. Sadly, empires, because of the resources they control, are capable of developing brash projects and visions. The people of Palestine lack those. But it was they who built those monuments with their sweat and hard labor. The empire provided "only" the ideas; the blueprints and plans. The actual physical labor was provided by the people of Palestine. Little has changed in the intervening centuries, as it is often cheap Palestinian labor and subcontractors who build the Israeli settlements in the West Bank. Why are the oppressed so often engaged in building and furthering the empire while they fail to erect their own infrastructure? For Jesus, the answer was lack of faith.

The most dangerous thing for the oppressed and occupied is that at some point they lose faith in themselves, in their ability to change the status quo. Faith is the key to dismantling the empire. Restoring people's confidence and faith is an important step toward liberation. It all starts in the brain. The oppressed have to begin thinking what seems to be the unthinkable. They have to know and realize that "yes, we can." The physical and other forms of confinement of the oppressed often lead to tunnel vision. Oppressed people are likely to stop imagining and stop developing bold ideas; they are caught up in the everyday struggle of providing the daily bread of survival. Reversing this dynamic is true resistance. True resistance is not killing a soldier or civilian or blowing up buildings. These are violent reactionary measures. Resistance is action, not reaction. Resistance requires faith, so it can stop being caught in the vicious cycle of retaliation that favors the powerful and tries to mirror it. Faith is nothing less than developing the bold vision of a new reality and mobilizing the needed resources to make it happen.

Jesus understood his mission not as a reaction to the Roman Empire but rather teaching that God's blueprint for the liberation of the people was to set them free and restore their faith in themselves and in God. One would think that the empire should be happy for such a constructive and nonviolent form of resistance. Yet, the opposite is often the case. The passage in Matthew concludes with Jesus telling his disciples, "The Son of Man is going to be betrayed into human hands, and they will kill him, and on the third day he will be raised" (Mt 17:22–23). Resistance has its price. It leads to the cross. The disciples should not have been surprised.

RESTORING THE COMMUNITY

Jesus knew only too well that one policy every empire utilizes is to "divide and conquer." He was referring to just such an imperial strategy when he said, "Every kingdom divided against itself becomes a desert, and house falls on house" (Lk 11:17). The unity of his people was thus something that concerned him. The fact that he called twelve disciples—to resemble the twelve tribes of Israel—was a clear indication that his mission was to restore the people and underline their unity. A look at the Twelve reveals them as people of diverse ideologies: a zealot, Simon (Mt 10:4), and a tax collector, Matthew (Mt 9:9); people who otherwise would not necessarily be grouped together. Among the Twelve were people from different regions of Palestine: Galilee, Iscariot, and Judea. Restoring a sense of community across ideological differences and geographical barriers is crucial for any community living under occupation. Occupied people often start to fight among themselves concerning the best way to resist the empire and consequently end up fighting one another instead of fighting the empire. As well, when people are confined by empires within small geographical areas, they begin to develop sub-identities, thus losing the sense of a communal identity. This is why Jesus invested his time in creating an inclusive community.

JESUS' POLITICAL PROGRAM

For people living under occupation and for people who are oppressed, the most important questions are: How can we be liberated? What is the way to freedom? What is the way to liberty? Jesus understood his mission as coming to liberate his people, which is why, in the Bible, he is called Savior. *Savior* is a Christian term for liberator. In order to understand Jesus' way in terms of liberation we first have to ask what paths he did *not* choose. Looking at Jesus' life, it is noteworthy that:

- Jesus never had a desire to go to Rome. This is fascinating because for somebody of his ability and standing the first thing to do to achieve liberation would seemingly be to head to Rome, just as Moses went to Pharaoh and said, "Let my people go!" Yet for Jesus, Rome and Caesar seemed to be utterly irrelevant.

- Jesus had no desire to create a political party. He could easily have done so, because the Gospels tell us that he was highly popular. Indeed, his popularity was greater than any other politician of his time. He had the opportunity to be king, and yet he had no desire to hold such a position. It might appear that Jesus was not a savvy politician: he couldn't seize the moment, he didn't use people to promote himself, he lost unique opportunities. Yet deciding not to create a political party was an important part of his strategy.

- Jesus had no desire whatsoever to be a religious leader, a chief rabbi, or a patriarch. He had the opportunity to become a leader of great renown, but he refused. Was Jesus, therefore, a bad politician? No. He simply had a different political agenda to liberate the people of Palestine.

So, what was his agenda? The following points give us some idea:

- Jesus was of the opinion that politics were too omnipresent in his day, an observation that I reiterate in the twenty-first century. Politics was the driving concern in people's minds. Yet with so much energy concentrated on politics, people neglected the *polis,* the city. Jesus understood that the equation was unbalanced; this explains why his political program basically consisted of traveling from one polis to the other, from one town to another, and from village to village (Mk 1:38–39). Jesus' program was to go precisely where no politician would ever tread, where no religious leader would ever head, that is, to the villages and remote towns whose names were barely known. In that sense Jesus was totally different from Paul. Paul was a strategist who had a vision to start a church in every major metropolis of the Roman Empire, creating a network of churches in each large town of the Roman Empire. That was Paul, the diaspora Jew, a strategist. Jesus was not interested in major towns; instead he opted for the remote villages of Palestine, and thus was always on a village tour. In fact, he was not even keen about Jerusalem; only toward the end of his life did he start traveling there. His entire ministry was devoted to the villages. People in the villages are the backbone of any important movement. It is not the intellectuals, not those living in the capitals developing theories about how to change the world who are at the heart of any liberation movement; rather, it is the people on the sidelines.

- At the center of Jesus' attention were the people of those villages, not himself—those who were marginalized, those who were possessed by demons, people who were not in control of their lives, people who had to fear for their lives, people who could not walk upright because they were under so much pressure and oppression. Jesus went to those villages and preached, taught, and healed. He went to places where people had almost no education, to people who had not received any attention, to people who had few, if any, opportunities. Jesus believed that liberation started with empowering those who were marginalized. There is no chance for any liberation or development to succeed until the hearts and minds of people in remote areas are reached.

Often, in situations of oppression, those who become educated and have the capacity to educate others end up educating people in the empire. When I look at the majority of young, highly educated Palestinians, who have something to contribute to their society, I witness them deciding to work abroad in the empire where there are millions like them; they end up employed by international organizations; they end up "preaching to the choir." Reaching out to the undeserved is often seen as something they have outgrown. They don't see themselves in that role anymore, believing they are called to a much higher mission. The consequence of this is that the gap between the empire and the periphery widens daily. The best and smartest of those who are oppressed get sucked into the empire. And those on the fringes are marginalized not solely by the empire, but indeed by their own people. Jesus wanted to restore their dignity so that they would start believing in themselves and see their calling. Jesus understood himself to be sent to the simple villagers of Palestine to whom he proclaimed the kingdom of God, sharing with them the vision of a kingdom that is much larger than Palestine.

AMBASSADORS FOR THE KINGDOM

Jesus spoke to the marginalized of a vision larger than Palestine and the state they had in mind, a vision even larger than Rome, something bigger than Caesar, and something stronger than the empire. He called this vision the kingdom of God. The most fascinating thing he told them was that God was calling them—those villagers of Palestine, those living on the margins of society. God was calling them to be the ambassadors of his kingdom. This is the vision that caught the attention of the people of Palestine. Such a vision must have been a stretch to those whose minds were mainly focused on the liberation of Palestine from the Romans and couldn't think of anything else. The liberation of Palestine was, for them, a bold enough vision. Their primary concern was how to restore the kingdom. For Jesus, the liberation of Palestine alone was never enough. Liberating a tiny piece of the empire was not the whole agenda. The vision had to be much grander, big enough to challenge the empire. The people of Palestine had to learn to think on a vast scale, they had to learn to leave room for God in the quest and process, and they had to learn to become part and parcel of representing God's vision on earth.

9

The Spirit

In the Middle East there is too much religion and too little spirituality. The most important questions for the Middle East today: What kind of spirit will prevail in the future in the region? What kind of culture will be predominant? Will it be the power of culture or the culture of power? The very soul of the people and of the region is at stake. What type of spirituality, therefore, is needed in the face of the empire?

NOT BY MIGHT

A big temptation for people living for decades under domination is that they become contaminated by the power of the empire. People who are subjected to state terror will start using terror, and people who experience continuous and systemic violence will ultimately become violent. The empire itself is corrupt, but it also corrupts those it controls.

"Not by might, nor by power, but by my spirit, says the Lord of hosts" (Zec 4:6). These words of the prophet Zechariah to Zerubbabel, the appointed governor of the province of Judah under Persian rule, are a prescient reminder to both the empire and those who act on its behalf. The alternate deception for any empire is to believe that military power is the master of all trades and solves all problems. That is a myth. In the last two decades the military intervention of the West in the Middle East, especially the wars in Afghanistan and Iraq, led nowhere and proved to be a total failure not only for the region, but also for the West. Yet the dominant mindset seems to think differently.

I recently had a discussion with a European ambassador. Among other things we spoke about Iran. He thought that a military strike against Iran was inevitable. I tried to argue that the last thing the region needs is another war. He looked at me as if I were the most radical or crazy person he had encountered. It is a sad and terribly strange commentary to live in an age where waging war becomes logical and where questioning war is seen as demented.

What is truly insane is to spend billions of dollars on arms and military equipment. Spending on military equipment comes at the cost of educating, empowering, and employing people. Regions are not safer with all of these weapons, which are mainly used by regimes against their own people, as has been the case in Libya, Syria, and many countries in the Middle East. The sales of weapons benefit only the empire and its military-industrial complex. It is past time to reconsider our priorities.

Thankfully, Palestine doesn't have and will never have the means to buy weapons and to put its resources into tools of destruction. Many are even calling for a demilitarized Palestine. It is said that approximately one-third of the development aid received by the Palestinian Authority is designated by donors for security, that is, ultimately the security of Israel. Defending the security of Israel is the pledge of every politician who wants to be elected or stay in power in the West.

DIVERSITY

The story of Pentecost (Acts 2:1–13) is imperative to understanding the spirituality that is needed in the Middle East because it provides a counter-narrative to the narrative of the empire. The narrative of the empire is found in Genesis (11:1–9), in the story of the Tower of Babel, where a mighty empire with a strong economy reaches to heaven and with one language holds the empire together. This is exactly what Alexander the Great and the Greeks tried to do in imposing Greek and Hellenistic culture on their conquered peoples. "Alexander and Company" had the ambitious plan to pour all tribes and groups into one gigantic melting pot. The outcome of this forceful unification was utter confusion. The empire fell apart and dissolved. The Romans tried the same experiment and were no more successful. Byzantine Emperor Constantine thought that by forcing one creed at Chalcedon, he could unite his empire behind one emperor and one faith. The Oriental identities and expressions of faith were thus declared heretical and were alienated. The ecumenical movement today, centuries later, is still suffering from this forceful unification. The Arabs tried to push their language onto the Berbers of North Africa and on central Asian countries. This led to the opposite effect: less identification with their empire by those tribes. The Soviets tried the same, and their empire too cracked and disintegrated.

This issue is central for the Middle East, which is pluralistic in nature. No single empire has been able to force the region into uniformity. There was never a single Catholic Church that monopolized the Christian faith in the Middle East, but rather national churches: Copts, Syriac, Marionites, Greeks, and so on, each worshiping in its own native language and possessing, as they do today, a distinct cultural identity. The same is true for Islam. It too has different expressions according to different regions: Shiite, Sunni, Alawite, Druze, and so forth. All efforts to unify them forcefully have come to naught. The Middle East continues to be one of the most diverse regions in the world, with multiple ethnicities, religious affiliations, and plural identities. For any empire this was and is both a challenge and an opportunity: a challenge, because the region resisted all attempts of forceful inclusion; an opportunity, because the empire was forever keen to play one group against the other and ensure that the region remained preoccupied with internecine fighting so that the empire's job of control was easier. This is part and parcel of colonial history in the Middle East. Prior to World War I the West assisted the Arabs against the Turks; today, the West is pitting Sunni Muslims against Shiite Muslims. Sometimes the West attempts to separate the Christians of the region from their Muslim neighbors.

In this context the story of Pentecost shows an alternative vision of the region by reversing the story of the Tower of Babel. Jerusalem becomes the counter-narrative of the empire. Here, on otherwise contested land, not far from the battleground, various nations and cultures meet. They don't speak the language of the empire, but rather their own native languages. Their identities are respected and embraced. The Spirit provides the software for communication so that they understand one another. In this story the rich diversity of the region is embraced and celebrated. It is regarded as strength rather than a deficiency. The multiple identities of the region are viewed not as contradictions, but as a treasure to save. In Jerusalem the people from the five regional empires mentioned earlier lived next to those who were oppressed by them, they "stood" on equal footing, "Parthians, Medes, Elamites, and residents of Mesopotamia, Judea and Cappadocia, Pontus and Asia, Phrygia and Pamphylia, Egypt and the parts of Libya belonging to Cyrene, and visitors from Rome, both Jews and proselytes, Cretans and Arabs" (Acts 2:9–10). The moment Pentecost was taken out of its original context, it became a nice story without any particular significance. It became a tale about speaking in tongues and thus lost its contextual relevance. The church born in Jerusalem was meant to counter the empire, not by creating another, but by providing a new, pluralistic Euro-Mediterranean vision. The spirituality so urgently needed today, more than at any previous time, is one that embraces diversity and pluralism and celebrates it as strength. The turbulent history of the Middle East is one of myriad national, racial, and religious minorities; countless refugees and displaced persons; and numerous tribes and clans. Without protecting the rights of all its minorities, there is no future for the Middle East.

MORE THAN VICTIMS

Pentecost was more than a vision. It provided a transformational experience for the disciples. After the Roman Empire executed Jesus, the disciples were understandably frightened. The movement created by him came to a standstill; its raison d'être seemed to have failed. It appeared that the empire had won. The resurrection didn't bring about change. Following the resurrection the disciples remained scared and behind closed doors. Only after receiving the Holy Spirit were they able to recover their courage and to focus again on their mission. The Spirit not only took their fear away but gave them a real sense for mission and direction.

If it were not for the resurrection, the disciples might have spent their entire lives mourning Jesus. It is so easy for the oppressed to dwell in mourning and almost revel in whining and self-pity. Without the Spirit the disciples would have continued life as usual in the shadow of the empire. One of the biggest temptations for oppressed people is feeling too comfortable in the role of the victim and to enter into a "blame game," cursing the empire. A major problem for victims of all empires is to identify so strongly with this role that they become double victims: victims of the empire, and victims of themselves.

Sometimes, when I hear some Jewish people talk, I feel as if they speak with a monopoly on victimhood. And sometimes I feel that some Palestinians feel that they must compete with the Jews over who is the greater victim. And sometimes when I read articles and books by Middle Eastern authors, I come across a conspiracy theory that makes the Arabs mere victims of the superpowers. It is both reassuring and comfortable to feel oneself a victim, because then one is neither responsible for the situation nor accountable. But even the weakest victim is also an actor who has to make choices and decisions—and assume responsibility. Simply blaming the empire doesn't help. In fact, it makes the victim feel more depressed, more helpless, and more hopeless. Playing the role of victim might assist those who are oppressed gain some sympathy but not necessarily respect.

On Pentecost it was the Spirit who enabled the disciples to overcome the notion of victimhood and to reach out as a people with a mission, as people who had something to say and something to contribute. Yes, they remained victims of the empire, but that was not their sole identity. Victimhood is a negative identity. The Spirit empowered the disciples to develop a positive identity, and consequently they ceased whining about their master who fell to the empire. Instead, they went out proclaiming the risen Christ, the former victim, now Lord, once dead and now alive. It is this Spirit who made history in Palestine. If the first disciples had gone forth blaming the empire and trying to elicit sympathy, Christianity would not have been born. If the first disciples had believed all that they had to share was the bad news of the cruelty of the empire, they would have remained unnoticed. The cruelty of the empire is not breaking news, and the world, dominated by the empire, is full of such news. The Spirit empowered the disciples to proclaim the good news, which was different from that of the empire. The disciples went out with the conviction that they had a message to share and that the world was waiting for just such a message. The world understood that if good news could hail from Palestine, then a miracle must have occurred. What the Middle East sorely needs today is this Spirit that helps people overcome their victimhood, assume responsibility, and undergo transformation from the status of objects in world history into subjects, actors, and positive contributors toward a new society. It is not enough that the Middle East gave the "Holy Books" to the world. The region must, in the twenty-first century, contribute something other than its oil reserves.

FREEDOM

One unique contribution that the people of Palestine and the Bible bring to the global table is the message of freedom. It is amazing to see how and in spite of almost three thousand years of imperial domination and occupation of the land of Palestine, the thirst for freedom remains alive and unquenched. None of the empires who ruled was able to crush this longing for freedom. The message of freedom didn't originate in the empire. Freedom there makes little sense. Only those who have endured a long history of occupation, who have lived all their lives in the shadow of the empires, know what true liberty means. It is not surprising that the message of freedom originated in Palestine. Today, the people of Palestine long for nothing more than freedom.

Freedom is what the masses in the Arab world today are yearning for. And yet it is striking to observe that the Middle East comes in last on the subject of human rights and individual freedom. Two forces are currently violating those rights: so-called security states that don't allow people to move, to have an opinion, to publish controversial books, to question policies, or simply to think critically; and religious movements that leave no room for people to choose their beliefs and to breathe freely. Both these contending forces in the Middle East share in their violation of the critically important value of freedom, and to that end both create systems based on fear. The fear of the state and the fear of God become two sides of the same coin. A society that is based on fear rather than on freedom kills the soul and spirit of its people, along with their capacity for innovation and creativity. There will be no true Arab Spring in the Middle East until we break out from the bondage of the security state as well as of oppressive "divine rights" to a wide open space where human lives and security are protected, where freedom is free to blossom, and where human rights become sacred.

WOMEN

Likewise, there is no future for the Middle East unless women are equal, free, educated, and fully enrolled in the labor market.[1] One of the exercises I like to do with young people in Palestine is to print on a piece of paper the following passage without identifying the source:

> A capable wife who can find?
>   She is far more precious than jewels.
> The heart of her husband trusts in her,
>   and he will have no lack of gain.
> She does him good, and not harm,
>   all the days of her life.
> She seeks wool and flax,
>   and works with willing hands.
> She is like the ships of the merchant,
>   she brings her food from far away.
> She rises while it is still night
>   and provides food for her household

and tasks for her servant-girls.
She considers a field and buys it;
    with the fruit of her hands she plants a
        vineyard.
She girds herself with strength,
    and makes her arms strong.
She perceives that her merchandise is profit-
    able.
    Her lamp does not go out at night.
She puts her hands to the distaff,
    and her hands hold the spindle.
She opens her hand to the poor,
    and reaches out her hands to the needy.
She is not afraid for her household when it
    snows,
    for all her household are clothed in crim-
    son.
She makes herself coverings;
    her clothing is fine linen and purple.
Her husband is known in the city gates,
    taking his seat among the elders of the
    land.
She makes linen garments and sells them;
    she supplies the merchant with sashes.
Strength and dignity are her clothing,
    and she laughs at the time to come.
She opens her mouth with wisdom,
    and the teaching of kindness is on her
    tongue.
She looks well to the ways of her household,
    and does not eat the bread of idleness.
Her children rise up and call her happy;
    her husband too, and he praises her:
"Many women have done excellently,

but you surpass them all."
Charm is deceitful, and beauty is vain,
  but a woman who fears the Lord is to be
    praised.
Give her a share in the fruit of her hands,
  and let her works praise her in the city.

I then ask the young people to discuss in small groups how they view the woman and to which century they would assign the text. The female depicted in the text is extremely hard-working, almost a super woman. In fact, one is forced to ask what her husband does other than "taking his seat among the elders of the land." By contrast, she is shown to work in the fields, growing food. She also knits, sews wool clothing, and embroiders. As a business- and tradeswoman she is involved in negotiating, selling, and buying, and she knows how to plan in the long term to secure the future of her household. Above all, she watches over her husband and children and takes good care of them. She heads the "family foundation," deciding on support to the poor and needy. She is mobile (certainly more than her husband!) and seems to be educated and wise. All these factors strike young people, who notice that cooking and cleaning are never mentioned as the exclusive virtues of a capable woman. They also note the patriarchal tone in the text; the man appears to be nothing but a judge, as if the woman works for him and he is her boss rather than her partner. Unsurprisingly, young people think that this text was written in the eighteenth or nineteenth century. The shock on their faces is palpable when they hear it was written at least twenty-five hundred years ago in Palestine and recorded in the Bible (Prv 31:10–31). They are astonished when I point to Palestinian village women today who continue to keep this culture alive: working in the fields, planting and harvesting, taking the produce of the field to the city each day, and walking house to house offering their vegetables, fruit, and dairy products for sale. These women constitute a major part of the Palestinian production force. We are mostly a consuming people. Palestinian women are the remnants of the production side of our economy. They are also maintaining bio-farming practices that have been neglected and inundated by a wave of non-organic Israeli products invading our markets.

From this perspective the situation of women in the Middle East over the last twenty-five hundred years has not improved; on the contrary, it has deteriorated. Whereas Palestine has moved from the Iron Age to postmodernity, the role of women in the region seems to have stepped backward: economically, culturally, religiously, and politically. As the result of continuous occupation, two developments have pushed the agenda of women onto the back burner. First, political liberation has always been regarded as the priority of the moment, the prevailing logic being that one has first to secure the liberation of the country and then work on liberating its women. In the absence of political liberation in the last twenty-five hundred years, the issue of women's liberation never became a serious part of the agenda. Second, because of the ongoing conflict the people of Palestine have often retreated to conservative forms of religion, which in turn have led to the suppression of the women. The question of women and their place in society was seldom seen as a priority. Middle Easterners continue to postpone the issue. Thus, women pay a double price—first, as a result of political conflict, and second, from conservative forms of religion. Yet, liberation is holistic. In its preoccupation with the empire, the region has missed the opportunity to work on self-improvement, challenging the patriarchal culture that is found within the occupied territories. It should be showing results in the area of women's liberation. Instead, we have lost the battle for liberating the land as well as the battle for liberating women. It is high time to reevaluate our priorities.

With the changes occurring in the region this specific task has today become ever more timely and pressing.

CREATIVE RESISTANCE

Resistance in a context of continuing occupation and oppression is omnipresent and will continue to play a role in Palestine as long as it is under occupation. The Arab Spring shows that resistance is spreading throughout the Middle East against regimes of oppression and corruption. The question, therefore, is not *whether* there should be resistance but *how* to resist. Resistance is a right, its framework having been established in the mid-twentieth century by international law. The twentieth century experienced two liberation movements that made nonviolent resistance a success: Gandhi's leadership in India against the British Empire, and Martin Luther King Jr.'s fight in the United States against racial discrimination and segregation. Both these movements managed to mobilize people to organize popular movements for their own liberation. Their success relied on recognizing the dangers in resorting to violence. They understood that violence is a culture unto itself; it is not something one dons like a hat when dealing with the "enemy" and then sets aside at the end of the confrontation. Once violence enters the arena, it creates a culture that is very difficult to eradicate. In fact liberation in the true sense also means liberating the "enemy" from its own violence. This is why nonviolence is often one of the most powerful tools in any resistance movement. In Palestine this type of resistance is increasingly becoming the cultural norm. The global BDS (boycott, divestment, and sanctions) campaign against Israel urges using these nonviolent tools against the occupation. These voices will grow in the future to confront an apartheid system that year after year becomes increasingly entrenched.

The Kairos Palestine document, written by a group of Palestinian Christians in 2009, crafted a new adjective to be added to resistance: *creative* resistance. Creative resistance goes one step further than nonviolent resistance. The word *nonviolence* is still a negation of a negative, and as such, for me, it leaves something to be desired. In my experience many of those supporting the nonviolence movement in Palestine unconsciously assume that Palestinians are violent people who need be taught to be nonviolent. State terror is seldom addressed. Representatives of an American organization once asked me support a project in education for nonviolence. I thanked them and said that I was absolutely for nonviolent resistance, but that I might have a better idea. I asked, "Why don't you think of doing a project in Israel teaching Israeli soldiers how to become nonviolent? They need that kind of training more than we do."

Creative resistance is important for another reason. One of the functions of any imperial ideology of occupation is to brand the conflict as if it were a conflict between a "civilized people," represented by the empire itself, and the "barbarians," who are dangerous not merely to the empire but to humanity. Continuing oppression is thus marketed as a virtue of the empire on behalf of humanity and its civilization and progress. Creative resistance specifically tackles this notion. It works on the branding of the narrative itself. This is of utmost importance because it questions the morality of the empire and confronts it with another narrative.

Last but not least, creative resistance is an important means of helping oppressed people to articulate their stories in new ways and forms. The question of liberation should not be expressed solely in political analyses that can become boring and inhuman. Our forefathers and foremothers were able to articulate their faith and resistance through stories and poetry.

We need a new generation that can express "the hopes and fears of all the years" through painting, dance, theater, and music. Giving the subaltern a voice to speak but also a face, a song, and a movement is the essence and product of creative resistance. This is the mission of Dar al-Kalima, the college that we started in Bethlehem in 2006, which focuses on music, art, dance, theater, and others fields that aim at developing the creative skills of our people.

CULTURE OF LIFE

In a context of oppression, martyrdom becomes a rallying symbol. In facing the Roman Empire many Christians and church leaders were killed for failing to submit to the power of the empire. The second-century church father Tertullian said, "The blood of the martyrs has become the seed for the church." The culture of martyrdom will continue to play a role as long as there is oppression. That culture of dying for one's country is a widespread cultural phenomenon, especially in imperial settings. Behind this culture is the notion that the death of a martyr is not in vain but part of a larger plan.

In the New Testament the death of Jesus is portrayed as a sacrifice. This has to be viewed as part of the cultural language of the time. And yet, there is something countercultural when Jesus' sacrifice is seen as the ultimate sacrifice for all time (Heb 9:12), which is why Paul repeatedly said that Jesus died so that we might live. Martyrs began to be associated with bearing witness through the offering of their life for a cause. The famous Palestinian Mahmoud Darwish, as I was delighted to discover, went through such a transformation from the theology of death to the theology of resurrection. He shifted from a theology of being ready to die for a belief to a theology of wanting to live for it. Dying for his country was not enough. There are already too many dead on all sides. A culture of life

is desperately needed today in the Middle East and throughout the world. Living for the community is necessary in the
twenty-first century so that "all may have life, and have it
abundantly" (Jn 10:10).

Epilogue:
Imagination and Hope

I was born in Bethlehem into a Palestinian Christian family. Palestine is my home, and Christianity is my faith. This is the land of my physical and spiritual ancestors. I was born under Jordanian rule and, at the age of five, experienced the beginning of the Israeli occupation of Bethlehem. I have just turned fifty years of age and have already witnessed nine wars. When Yasser Arafat and Yitzhak Rabin shook hands at the White House in 1993, I thought that the Israelis and Palestinians would finally live together in peace.

Today, I fear for my two daughters, Dana and Tala, and wonder whether they will ever experience peace during their lifetimes. But I am convinced that war is not destiny. After all, in the midst of the Roman occupation the angels proclaimed peace on earth. Peace in the Holy Land must be the mandate for all of us. We cannot abandon responsibility for our fellow human beings. Engaged responsibility belongs to mature citizens and is crucial for a civil society to function and thrive.

I know that many have given up on peace in the Middle East. Many have tried their best but to no avail. I would argue that the world has been managing the conflict rather than solving it. The peace model that has been employed to date has been a type of Pax Romana where the empire dictates peace either through endless processes or through facts on the ground (settlements, land confiscation, colonization, and so forth), thus buying time to expand the boundaries of the empire. Pax Romana was rejected by the Judeans of the first century, and similar models are understandably rejected by the Palestinians of the twenty-first century.

Peace dictated by the empire is not desirable, doable, or durable. Is peace with the empire, therefore, ever truly possible? Our forefathers and foremothers in the Bible struggled with this critical question repeatedly and developed diverse answers. Some authors, such as Deutero-Isaiah, saw the empire as a tool in the hand of God fulfilling his will (Is 45:1–4); others saw the empire as the ultimate axis of evil that God would destroy completely (Rv 18). And Trito-Isaiah imagines the unimaginable:

> The wolf and the lamb shall feed together,
>   the lion shall eat straw like the ox;
>   but the serpent—its food shall be dust.
> (Is 65:25)

Here a new Middle Eastern reality is envisioned: the wolf (a code for the empire) will be domesticated and no longer harm the lamb, while the lion (a code for the superpower) will be tamed and will eat straw like an ox. A new reality is envisioned whereby the empire will disarm and will cease to put its faith and its resources in military spending but rather will live peacefully.

Is this just an illusion, wishful thinking, or a hallucination? I believe not. All life in general, and life in the Holy Land in particular, is a matter of living in the tension between the "the world as it is" with all its ugly and painful realities and the "the world as it could be." We have to balance that tension. Being too absorbed by "the world as it is" makes us resentful. Dreaming too much about "the world as it should be" makes us naive and passive. We must live with our feet firmly grounded in the reality of this world with its empires, yet, at the same time, be engaged in creating with our own hands a foretaste of the kingdom to come. We have to learn to hold the reins of the tension between history with its endless injuries and the vision of a future with its promises, ever conscious that the present is the space to heal wounds and to seize opportunities. We need to analyze the patterns of the past without falling into a kind of fatalism whereby we become objects of history. For we lose the future the moment we lose our capability for imagination. Without faith, there is no imagination; without imagination, there is no innovation; and without innovation, there is no future. Faith embodies the view that we can imagine something that was not, until the present, part of our history. It is of utmost importance for the people of the Middle East to develop a new vision for their region. To date, such vision is precisely what is lacking in the so-called Arab Spring.

Our biblical ancestors envisioned a land stretching "from the river of Egypt to the great river, the river Euphrates" (Gn 15:18). Some evangelical Christians believe that these two waterways should be the ultimate boundaries of a greater Israel. Some have viewed the two blue lines on the Israeli flag to symbolize these two great rivers. Such ambitions are part of an imperial expansionist agenda. But if we take the geopolitics of the Middle East discussed earlier, where Palestine has always been torn between neighboring empires and used either as a buffer zone or as battlefield, the vision from the Nile to the Euphrates seen from the perspective of the people of the land, not from the empire, would mean that Palestine is like a bird with two wings: one wing is Egypt to the south, and the other wing is Syria and Iraq to the north. A bird can't fly without synchronizing its wings. The failure of Camp David in 1979 was that it couldn't get the two wings to agree, to be part of the deal. The players involved thought that the bird could fly with one wing. That was perhaps the single pivotal lost opportunity. It was also the failure of Oslo. For the people of Palestine, the vision must be regional. It has to incorporate neighboring regional powers, including the smaller countries of Jordan and Lebanon who share, to some extent, the destiny of Palestine. It is in these larger areas between the two rivers that the people of Palestine used to move, to seek refuge, and to conduct business. It is in this region that all of biblical history took place. The area from the Nile to the Euphrates today is a region in turmoil. We are not sure what will happen in Syria, Egypt, Iraq, Lebanon, or even in Jordan and Palestine. We might be entering a dark tunnel of uncertainty, violence, and chaos. It is thus even more important that imaginative vision is developed.[1] One has to think of including the Euro-Mediterranean region as a whole in such an imaginative vision. I know that this might sound out of touch with reality. But that is precisely my point—the reason why imaginative vision is so sorely needed. We have to learn how to think what now seems to be unthinkable.

The problem of the region is also the problem of the people of Palestine, who could not and cannot think big enough. More often the peoples of the region are obsessed with narrow agendas that they perceive to be important for their country, and consequently they miss seeing the larger picture. The region of the Middle East is not necessarily poor, but it is impoverished by the policies of those in power, by the continuing Israeli-Palestinian conflict, and by the imperial exploitation of its natural as well as its human resources. Can we imagine a new Middle East? Can the peoples of the Middle East imagine a new Middle East? Can we do it now, in the course of the so-called Arab Spring, when everything seems to be falling apart within subcultures and sectarian groups? Can we do it at a time when imperial powers are trying to draw lines for a new Middle East that is not necessarily in the interest of the people themselves? I believe that because of all of these factors a new vision by the people and for the people is no longer a luxury but an absolute necessity. Without a new driving vision and without allowing for such an imaginative process to take place, the region will spiral into chaos. "Where there is no vision, the people perish" (Prv 29:18, KJV). It is in this very context of the so-called Arab Spring, when many regional and international powers are trying to pull and push the region in disparate directions, that the region has to stop and ponder what future it envisions for its children. It is in this time of immense challenges that imaginative faith rises to discover the endless possibilities that lie herein. Faith as imaginative power is put to the test "for such a time as this" (Est 4:14). Only a bold vision can pull the region out of its current chaos. Only if we are able to reimagine the region anew will our people have life and have it abundantly. Like people everywhere, those who have been demonstrating on the streets of the Arab world have no other desire but to have life and a future; to enjoy freedom, dignity, and equality; to have work and stability; and to be able to tap into endless opportunities.

While the political analysts remind us of the immense challenges facing Palestine and the region, imagination shows us the endless opportunities that are within reach. The bridge between immense challenges and endless opportunities is hope in action. Imagination is what we see. Hope is putting what we see into action today. Hope is the power to keep focusing on the larger vision while taking the small, often undramatic, steps toward that future. Imagination can be highly deceptive if it is not connected to a well-defined strategy and a plan. Hope doesn't wait for vision to appear. Hope is vision in action today. Faith that makes people passive, depressive, or delusional is not faith but opium. We have a great deal of that in our region and the world today. Faith is facing the empire with open eyes that allow us to analyze what is happening while, at the same time, developing the ability to see beyond our present capacities. Hope is living the reality and yet investing in a different one. The Jerusalemite prophet Jeremiah is the incarnation of this biblical hope. When his city was burned and the Temple where he was serving destroyed, all hope seemed to be lost. Yet Jeremiah, himself in prison, was asked by a cousin to buy from him a field near Jerusalem (Jer 32:1–15). Jeremiah did so. He was able to imagine a future beyond the destruction around him. But that alone was not hope. Hope was deciding to invest in the area at a time when no sane person would so dare. Hope is faith in action in the face of the empire. Hope is what we do today. Only that which we do today as people of faith and as engaged citizens can change the course of history and lay the foundation for a different future. This was the prophetic tradition that came out of Palestine, a tradition we must keep alive.

Notes

INTRODUCTION

1. For more on the decline of the Palestinian Christian community, see Rania Al Qass Collings, Rifat Odeh Kassis, and Mitri Raheb, eds., *Palestinian Christians in the West Bank: Facts, Figures, and Trends* (Bethlehem: Diyar, 2012); and Johnny Mansour, ed., *Arab Christians in Israel: Facts, Figures, and Trends* (Bethlehem: Diyar 2012).

2. R. S. Sugirtharajah, *Troublesome Texts: The Bible in Colonial and Contemporary Culture* (Sheffield: Phoenix Press 2008), 104–5.

3. Five conferences have been organized by Diyar in Bethlehem. The titles of these conferences are "Shaping Communities in Times of Crises: Narratives of Land, People, and Identities" in 2005; "God's Reign and People's Rule: Religious Communities, Political Entities, and Civil Societies in Palestine" in 2007; "The Invention of History: A Century of Interplay Between Theology and Politics in Palestine" in 2009; "Biblical Texts, Ur-Contexts, and Contemporary Realities in Israel and Palestine: The Interplay Between Biblical Hermeneutics and Modern Politics" in 2011; and "Palestinian Identity in Relation to Time and Space: A Dialogue Between Theology, Archeology, and the Arts" in 2013.

I. HISTORY AND THE BIBLICAL STORY

1. *Longue durée* is an expression used by the French Annales School of historic writing that gives priority to long-term historical structures over events.

2. Mitri Raheb, "Displacement Theopolitics," in *The Invention of History: A Century of Interplay Between Theology and Politics in Palestine,* ed. Mitri Raheb (Bethlehem: Diyar, 2011), 16.

3. Ber Borochov, "On the Issue of Zion and the Territory," in *Works* (Tel Aviv: Hakibbutz Hameuhad, 1955 [Hebrew]), 1:148, quoted in Shlomo Sand, *The Invention of the Jewish People* (London: Verso, 2009), 184–85.

4. David Ben Gurion and Yitzhak Ben-Zvi, *Eretz Yisrael in the Past and Present* (Jerusalem: Ben-Zvi, 1979 [Hebrew]), 196, quoted in ibid., 185.

5. Quoted in ibid., 186, 184.

6. Philip Davies, *Memories of Ancient Israel* (Louisville, KY: Westminster, 2008), 106.

7. The Arabic word *nakba* literally means "catastrophe." It refers to the year 1948, when the Palestinians lost over 77 percent of their land to Israel, thus becoming refugees.

8. Globalfirepower.com ranks Israel as tenth in the world, excluding its nuclear power capability. When taking its nuclear power capabilities into consideration, Israel ranks seventh.

9. Jan Assmann, *Moses the Egyptian: The Memory of Egypt in Western Monotheism* (Cambridge, MA: Harvard University Press, 1997), 14.

10. Shlomo Sand, *The Invention of the Jewish People* (London: Verso, 2009).

11. Mitri Raheb, "Displacement Theopolitics," 19.

12. Ibid., 21.

13. A good summary is provided by Kevin Chamberlain, "Stealing Palestinian History," *This Week in Palestine* (June 2013). Available on the thisweekinpalestine.com websute.

14. Mitri Raheb, "Displacement Theopolitics," 22.

15. Ilan, Pappe, *The Ethnic Cleansing of Palestine* (Oxford: Oneworld Publications, 2006).

16. Ibid.

17. Davies, *Memories of Ancient Israel,* 11.

18. Rafiq Khoury, "The Conflict of Narratives: From Memory to Prophecy," in *The Invention of History: A Century of Interplay Between Theology and Politics in Palestine,* ed. Mitri Raheb (Bethlehem: Diyar, 2011), 266.

19. Davies, *Memories of Ancient Israel*, 11.

2. A PRELUDE TO A PALESTINIAN NARRATIVE

1. John J. Mearsheimer and Stephen M. Walt, *The Israel Lobby and US Foreign Policy* (New York: Farrar, Straus, and Giroux, 2007).

2. Larry Eskridge, "Defining Evangelicalism," Institute for the Study of American Evangelicals (ISAE) (1996, rev. 2012). Available on the wheaton.edu website.

3. Julia O'Brien, "The Hermeneutical Predicament," in *Biblical Text in the Context of Occupation*, ed. Mitri Raheb (Bethlehem: Diyar, 2012), 169–70.

4. Alex Kane, "Jewish Establishment Pulls Out of Interfaith Dialogue, Threatens Congressional Investigation of Delegitimizers over Christian Letter," *Mondoweiss* (October 17, 2012). Available on the mondoweiss.net website.

5. Edward Said, *Orientalism* (New York: Random House, 1978).

6. Bill Ashcroft, *Post-Colonial Studies: The Key Concepts* (New York: Routledge, 2007). There are many excellent web sources on this issue: postcolonialweb.org; postcolonial.org; and Deepika Bahri, "Postcolonial Studies at Emory," english .emory.edu website.

7. R. S. Sugirtharajah, *The Postcolonial Bible,* Bible and Postcolonialism series, vol. 1 (Sheffield: Sheffield Academic Press, 1998), 15.

8. Mitri Raheb, *I Am a Palestinian Christian* (Minneapolis: Augsburg-Fortress, 1995), 28–34.

9. Al-Liqa' Center established a conference entitled "Theology and the Local Church in the Holy Land" in 1987 for the purpose of formulating a local response within an ecumenical context in Palestine. This conference produced the "Basic Document on Theology and the Local Church." See Ulrike Bechmann, *Vom Dialog zur Solidarität. Das christlich-islamische Gespräch in Palästina* (Trier: Aphorisma, 2000). The second center, the Sabeel Centre for Liberation Theology, was established in 1989 by Rev. Naim Ateek. "Sabeel is an ecumenical grassroots liberation theology movement among Palestinian Christians. Inspired by the life and teaching of Jesus Christ, this liberation theology seeks to deepen the faith of Palestinian Christians, promote unity among

them, and lead them to social action." For more, see the sabeel.org. website. And finally, Dar Annadwa Addawliyyah/Diyar was established in 1995 with the aim of equipping the local community to assume an active role in shaping its future. Developing a Christian theology for the Palestinian context, supporting the emergence of contextual Palestinian Christian art and music, and organizing international theological encounters soon became three distinct foci for Dar Annadwa. For more, see the diyar.ps website.

10. Keith Whitelam, *The Invention of Ancient Israel: The Silencing of Palestinian History* (New York: Routledge, 1996).

11. Ralph Broadbent, "Postcolonial Biblical Studies in Action: Origins and Trajectories," in *Exploring Postcolonial Biblical Criticism: History, Method, Practice,* ed. R. S. Sugirtharajah, 57–93 (Malden, MA: Blackwell Publishing, 2012), 61.

12. Ibid., 57–93.

13. Robert Allen Warrior, "A North American Perspective: Canaanites, Cowboys, and Indians," in *Voices from the Margin: Interpreting the Bible in the Third World*, ed. R. S. Sugirtharajah (Maryknoll, NY: Orbis Books, 1991), 289.

14. Kwok Pui-Ian, *Discovering the Bible in the Non-Biblical World* (Maryknoll, NY: Orbis Books, 1995), 99.

15. Michael Prior, *The Bible and Colonialism: A Moral Critique* (Sheffield: Academic Press, 1997), 11.

16. A new generation of Palestinian Christian evangelical theologians is emerging, represented by scholars such as Yohanna Katanacho, Munther Isaac, and others. See the christatthecheckpoint. com website.

17. Marc Ellis's *Towards a Jewish Theology of Liberation* (Maryknoll, NY: Orbis Books, 1987) became an expression of this yearning for liberating Israel from itself. His other titles also express this yearning (see, e.g., *Judaism Does Not Equal Israel: The Rebirth of the Jewish Prophetic* [New York: New Press, 2009]).

18. Uri Davis, *Israel: An Apartheid State* (London: Zed Books, 1987).

19. Shlomo Sand, *The Invention of the Jewish People* (London: Verso, 2009), 73.

20. Shlomo Sand, *The Invention of the Land of Israel: From Holy Land to Homeland* (London: Verso, 2012).

21. Walter Brueggemann, *The Land* (Philadelphia: Fortress Press, 1977).

22. Walter Brueggemann, *The Land: Place as Gift, Promise, and Challenge in Biblical Faith*, 2nd ed. (Minneapolis: Fortress Press, 2002).

23. Ibid., xiii–xiv.

24. David Jasper, *A Short Introduction to Hermeneutics* (Louisville, KY: Westminster, 2004), 123–24, 125.

25. Norman Gottwald, "Early Israel as an Anti-Imperial Community," in Horsley, *In the Shadow of the Empire,* 24.

26. See, among others, Grace Halsell, Victoria Clark, Nur Masalha, Klifford Attick Kiracofe, Stephen Sizer, and Robert Smith. See also, the christianzionism.org website.

27. Halvor Moxnes, Ward Blanton, and James G. Crossley, eds., "Introduction," *Jesus Beyond Nationalism: Constructing the Historical Jesus in a Period of Cultural Complexity* (London: Equinox, 2009), 5–6.

28. Halvor Moxnes, *Jesus and the Rise of Nationalism: A New Quest for the Nineteenth-Century Historical Jesus* (New York: Tauris, 2012), 1.

29. Kairos Palestine, "A Moment of Truth: A Word of Faith, Hope, and Love from the Heart of Palestinian Suffering" (Bethlehem: Kairos Palestine, 2009). Available on thekairospalestine.ps website.

30. Ibid.

3. THE MIDDLE EAST

1. Huseyin Yilmaz, "The Eastern Question and the Ottoman Empire: The Genesis of the Near and Middle East in the Nineteenth Century," in *Is There a Middle East? The Evolution of a Geopolitical Concept*, ed. Michael E. Bonine, Abbas Amanat, and Michael Ezekiel Gasper, 11–35 (Palo Alto, CA: Stanford University Press, 2012), 34.

2. Bonine, Amanat, and Gasper, *Is There a Middle East?* 240.

3. Marc Van De Mieroop, *A History of the Ancient Near East ca. 3000–323 BC* (Malden, MA: Blackwell Publishing, 2007), 3.

4. Ibid., 130.

4.   PALESTINE

1.   Marc Van De Mieroop, *A History of the Ancient Near East ca. 3000–323 BC* (Malden, MA: Blackwell Publishing, 2007), 129.

2.   For more detail, see Salim Tamari, *Mountain Against the Sea: Essays on Palestinian Society and Culture* (Berkeley and Los Angeles: University of California Press, 2009).

5.   THE EMPIRE

1.   United Nations Office for the Coordination of Humanitarians Affairs (UN OCHA), "Movement and Access in the West Bank" (September 27, 2011). The Israel Human Rights Organization, B'tselem, talks about ninety-eight fixed Israeli checkpoints inside the West Bank—fifty-seven separating Palestinian towns, and forty-one inside the West Bank as crossings into Israel—in addition to around 351 "flying checkpoints" every month. The UN report is available on theunispal.un.org website.

2.   The separation wall is, an average, twenty to thirty feet high. Over 90 percent of it is constructed inside the West Bank on Palestinian land, thus violating international law. Approximately two-thirds of it is already constructed. It includes electronic fences, barbed-wire fences, and trenches. See B'tselem, "Separation Barrier—Statistics (January 1, 2011; updated July 15, 2012). available on the btselem.org website. See also, International Court of Justice, "Legal Consequiences of the Construction of a Wall in the Occupied Palestinian Territory: Summary of the Advisory Opinion of 8 July 9, 2004." Available on the icj-cij.org websitef.

3.   The water resources of the Palestinian Occupied Territory are used by Israel, in violation of international law, for the benefit of Jewish settlers over native Palestinians. B'tselem, "The Water Crisis" (January 1, 2011). Available on the btselem.org website.

4.   See Iain Scobbie and Alon Margalit, "The Israeli Military Commander's Powers under the Law of Occupation in Relation to Quarrying Activity in Area C," Diakonia (July 4, 2012); "Pillage of the Dead Sea: Israel's Unlawful Exploitation of Natural Resources in

the Occupied Palestinian Territory," *Al-Haq* (September 3, 2012); for the situation in Gaza, see UNISPAL, "Farming Without Land, Fishing Without Water: Gaza Agricultural Sector Struggles to Survive," Unispal (May 2010); for the situation in the West Bank, see Hanan Chehata, "A Harvest of Tears: Palestinian Agriculture Continues to Suffer as a Result of Ruthless Israeli Policies," *Middle East Monitor* (March 16, 2013). For an example pertaining to the Old City of Jerusalem, see Yonathan Mizrachi, "Between Holiness and Propaganda" (Jerusalem: Emek Shaveh, December 2011). Available on the alt-arch.org website.

5. For a good overview of the history and ideology of settlements, see Idith Zertal and Akiva Eldar, *Die Herren des Landes: Israel und die Siedlerbewegung seit 1967* (Munich: DVA, 2007). For settlement statistics, see the Foundation for Middle East Peace, "Settlement Information" (March 16, 2013). Available on the fmep.orgwebsite.

6. Rafi Segal and Eyal Weizmann, eds., *A Civilian Occupation: The Politics of Israeli Architecture* (London: Verso, 2003).

7. For a full analysis, see Walid Khalidi, *All That Remains: The Palestinian Villages Occupied and Depopulated by Israel in 1948* (Washington, DC: Insitute of Palestine Studies, 2006); Rochelle A. Davis, *Palestinian Village Histories: Geographies of the Displaced* (Palo Alto, CA: Stanford University Press, 2011). For a list of the 418 villages, see *Palestine-Israel Journal, a Focus of 1948–1998* (Washington, DC: Institute of Palestine Studies, 2006).

8. Ami Isserhoff, "Deir Yassin: The Evidence" (July 13, 2012). Available on the israel-palestina.info website.

9. According to the 2012 Palestinian Initiative for the Promotion of Global Dialogue and Democracy (MIFTAH), the number of Palestinians imprisoned by Israel since 1967 is around 750,000, representing approximately 20 percent of the total Palestinian population in the Palestinian Occupied Territories to date. For more on the issue of prisoners, see the miftah.org website.

10. See Brad E. Kells, Frank Ritchey Ames, and Jacob Life Wright, *Interpreting Exile: Displacement and Deportation in Biblical and Modern Contexts* (Atlanta: Society of Biblical Literature, 2011).

11. John Bunzl, *Israel und die Palaestinenser: Die Entwicklung eines Gegensatzes* (Vienna: Wilhelm Braumueller, 1982), 49–57.

12. For more on the refugee issue, see the unrwa.org website and the badil.org website. See also Benny Morris, *The Birth of the Palestinian Refugee Problem Revisited* (Cambridge: Cambridge University Press, 2004).

13. See the ongoing comparative, historical, and social studies at the University of California at Berkeley: Michael Man, *The Sources of Social Power* (Cambridge: Cambridge University Press), vol. 1, *A History of Power from the Beginning to AD 1760* (1986); vol. 2, *The Rise of Classes and Nation-State, 1760–1914* (1993). John Crossan calls imperial theology the "ideological glue" that holds the empire together. See John Dominic Crossan, "Roman Imperial Theology," in *In the Shadow of Empire: Reclaiming the Bible as a History of Faithful Resistance,* ed. Richard Horsely, 59–74 (Louisville, KY: Westminster John Knox Press, 2008).

14. See J. A. Loubser, *Critical Review of Racial Theology in South Africa: The Apartheid Bible* (New York: Edwin Mellen Press, 1991); George E. Tinker, *Missionary Conquest: The Gospel and Native American Cultural Genocide* (Minneapolis: Augsburg-Fortress, 1993); and Norman C. Habel, *Reconciliation: Searching for Australia's Soul* (Sydney: HarperCollins, 1999).

6. THE PEOPLE OF PALESTINE

1. For eyewitness reports, see the eappi.org website.

2. Mitri Raheb, *Bethlehem Besieged* (Minneapolis: Augsburg-Fortress, 2004), 27–34.

3. I am aware that there were different groups then, such as the fifth philosophy, the Sicarri, the Zealots, and several groups today as well. See Martin Hengel, *Die Zeloten: Untersuchungen zur jüdischen Freiheitsbewegung in der Zeit von Herodes* (Tübingen: Mohr Siebeck 2011). Also see Richard A. Horsley with John A. Hanson, *Bandits, Prophets, and Messiahs: Popular Movements in the Time of Jesus* (Harrisburg, PA: Trinity Press International, 1992); and Jacob Neusner, *Origins of Judaism: The Pharisees and Other Sects*, vol. 2, part 2 (New York: Garland, 1990).

4. Horsley, *Bandits, Prophets, and Messiahs*, 223.

5. Examples include 40–37 BC, 4–1 BC, AD 66–70, AD 132–35, 1936–39, 1987–91, 2000–2004.

6. See, for example, Josua Hammer, *A Season in Bethlehem: Unholy War in a Sacred Place* (New York: Free Press, 2003).

7. See Jacob Z. Lauterbach, "The Pharisees and Their Teachings", in Neusner, *Origins of Judaism,* 57–129.

8. Ibid., 101–2.

9. Jodi Magness, *The Archeology of Qumran and the Dead Sea Scrolls* (Grand Rapids, MI: Eerdmans, 2002).

10. See United Nations, "General Assembly Votes Overwhelmingly to Accord Palestine 'Non-member Observer State' Status in United Nations," GA/11317 (November 29, 2012). Available on the un.org website.

7.   GOD

1. Jacob Wrights argues that the literature of the Hebrew Bible underwent its most significant formulation in contexts of defeat and that the national identity of the people of Palestine was constructed in response to that. See Jacob Wright, "The Commemoration of Defeat and the Formation of a Nation in the Hebrew Bible," Proof 29 (2009): 433–72.

8.   JESUS

1. Richard A. Horsley, "Jesus and Empire," in *In the Shadow of Empire: Reclaiming the Bible as a History of Faithful Resistance* (Louisville, KY: Westminster John Knox Press, 2008), 76–77.

9.   THE SPIRIT

1. For more on the situation of women in the Middle East, see United Nations Development Programme, "The Arab Human Development Report 2005: Towards the Rise of Women in the Arab World" (2005). Available on the arab-hdr.org website.

10.   EPILOGUE

1. The organization I founded and which I still head, Diyar, started a program called "Seizing the Moment: Envisioning a Middle East for Tomorrow." For more information, see the diyar.ps website.

Selected Bibliography

Ashcroft, Bill. *Post-Colonial Studies: The Key Concepts.* New York: Routledge, 2007.

Ateek, Naim. *Challanging Christian Zionism: Theology, Politics, and the Israel-Palestine Conflict.* London: Melisende, 2005.

————. *Faith and the Intifada: Palestinian Christian Voices.* Maryknoll, NY: Orbis Books, 1992.

————. *Holy Land Hollow Jubilee: God, Justice, and the Palestinians.* London: Melisende, 1999.

————. *Justice and Only Justice: A Palestinian Theology of Liberation.* Maryknoll, NY: Orbis Books, 1989.

————. *A Palestinian Cry for Reconciliation.* Maryknoll, NY: Orbis Books, 2008.

Bahri, Deepika. "Postcolonial Studies at Emory." 1996. http://www.english.emory.edu/Bahri/Intro.html.

Bechmann, Ulrike. *Vom Dialog zur Solidarität. Das christlich-islamische Gespräch in Palästina.* Trier: Aphorisma, 2000.

Bethlehem Bible College. "Christ at the Checkpoint," Conference. November 3, 2012. http://www.christatthecheckpoint.com/.

Bonine, Michael E., Abbas Amanat, and Michael Ezekiel Gasper. *Is There a Middle East? The Evolution of a Geopolitical Concept.* Palo Alto, CA: Stanford University Press, 2012.

Broadbent, Ralph. "Postcolonial Biblical Studies in Action: Origins and Trajectories." In Sugirtharajah, *Exploring Postcolonial Biblical Criticism,* 57–93.

Every effort has been made to ensure that the URLs in this book are accurate and up to date. However, where URLs no longer operate, readers may use one of the numerous search engines available on the Internet to access the information they seek.

Brueggemann, Walter. "Faith in the Empire." In Horsley, *In the Shadow of Empire*, 25–40.

———. *Out of Babylon*. Nashville, TN: Abingdon Press, 2010.

B'tselem. "Restriction of Movement." July 16, 2012. http://www.btselem.org/freedom_of_movement/checkpoints_and_forbidden_roads.

———. "Separation Barrier." B'tselem. July 16, 2012. http://www.btselem.org/separation_barrier/statistics.

———. "The Water Crisis." B'tselem. January 1, 2011. http://www.btselem.org/water.

Bunzl, John. *Israel und die Palaestinenser: Die Entwicklung eines Gegensatzes.* Vienna: Wilhelm Braumueller, 1982.

Burge, Gary. *Jesus and the Land: The New Testament Challenge to Holy Land Theology.* Grand Rapids, MI: Baker Academic, 2010.

———. *Who Are God's People in the Middle East?* Grand Rapids, MI: Zondervan, 1993.

———. *Whose Land? Whose Promise? What Christians Are Not Being Told About Israel and the Palestinians.* Cleveland: Pilgrim Press, 2003.

Carter, Waren. *Matthew and Empire: Initial Explorations.* Harrisburg, PA: Trinity Press International, 2001.

———. *The Roman Empire and the New Testament: An Essential Guide.* Nashville, TN: Abingdon Press, 2006.

Chacour, Elias. *Blood Brothers.* Grand Rapids, MI: Chosen Books, 1984.

———. *We Belong to the Land.* Notre Dame, IN: University of Notre Dame Press, 2001.

Chamberlain, Kevin. *This Week in Palestine.* June 2013. http://thisweek-inpalestine.com/details.php?id=1451&ed=107.

Chehata, Hanan. "A Harvest of Tears: Palestinian Agriculture Continues to Suffer as a Result of Ruthless Israeli Policies." *Middle East Monitor.* October 19, 2011. http://www.middleeastmonitor.com/reports/by-dr-hanan-chehata/2959–a-harvest-of-tears-palestinian-agriculture-continues-to-suffer-as-a-result-of-ruthless-israeli-policies.

Clark, Victoria. *Allies for Armageddon: The Rise of Christian Zionism.* New Haven, CT: Yale University Press, 2007.

Crossan, John Dominic. "Roman Imperial Theology." In Horsley, *In the Shadow of Empire*, 59–74.

Crossley, James G. *Jesus in an Age of Terror: Scholarly Projects for a New American Century.* London: Equinox, 2008.

Davies, Philip R. *Memories of Ancient Israel: An Introduction to Biblical History—Ancient and Modern.* Louisville, KY: Westminster, 2008.

Davis, Rochelle A. *Palestinian Village Histories: Geographies of the Displaced.* Stanford, CA: Stanford University Press, 2011.

Davis, Uri. *Israel: An Apartheid State.* (London: Zed Book, 1987).

El-Assal, Riah Abu. *Caught in Between: The Extraordinary Story of an Arab Palestinian Christian Israeli.* London: SPCK, 1999.

Ellis, Marc. *Towards a Jewish Theology of Liberation.* Maryknoll, NY: Orbis Books, 1987.

Foundation for Middle East Peace. "Settlement Information." March 16, 2013. http://www.fmep.org/settlement_info.

Gasper, Michael Ezekiel. "There Is a Middle East!" In Bonine, Amanat, and Gasper, *Is There a Middle East?* 231–42.

Gottwald, Norman. "Early Israel as an Anti-Imperial Community." In Horsley, *In the Shadow of Empire*, 9–24.

Habel, Norman C. *Reconciliation: Searching for Australia's Soul.* Sydney: HarperCollins, 1999.

Haj, Nadia Abu El. *Facts on the Ground: Archaeological Practice and Territorial Self-Fashioning in Israeli Society.* Chicago: University of Chicago Press, 2001.

Halsell, Grace. *Prophecy and Politics: Militant Evangelists on the way to Nuclear War.* Westport, CT: Lawrence Hill Books, 1989.

———. *Prophecy and Politics: The Secret Alliance between Israel and the US Christian Right.* Chicago: Lawrence Hill Books, 1989.

Hammer, Josua. *A Season in Bethlehem: Unholy War in a Sacred Place.* New York: Free Press, 2003.

Hengel, Martin. *Die Zeloten: Untersuchungen zur juedischen Freiheitsbewegung in der Zeit von Herodes.* Tübingen: Mohr Siebeck, 2011.

Horsley, Richard A. *Jesus and Empire: The Kingdom of God and the New World Disorder.* Minneapolis: Fortress Press, 2002.

———. *Paul and the Roman Imperial Order.* Harrisburg, PA: Trinity Press International, 2004.

———. *Religion and Empire: People, Power, and the Life of the Spirit.* Minneapolis: Fortress Press, 2003.

————, ed. *In the Shadow of Empire: Reclaiming the Bible as a History of Faithful Resistance.* Louisville, KY: Westminster John Knox Press, 2008.

Horsley, Richard A., and John A. Hanson. *Bandits, Prophets and Messiahs: Popular Movements in the Time of Jesus.* Harrisburg, PA: Trinity, 1999.

International Court of Justice. "Legal Consequences of the Construction of a Wall in the Occupied Palestinian Territory." July 9, 2004. http://www.icj-cij.org/docket/files/131/1677.pdf.

Isserhoff, Ami. "Deir Yassin: The Evidence." The Israel-Palestina Info. July 13, 2012. http://www.israel-palestina.info/deir-yassin -the-evidence/.

Jasper, David. *A Short Introduction to Hermeneutics.* Louisville, KY: Westminster, 2004.

Kairos Palestine. "A Moment of Truth: A Word of Faith, Hope, and Love from the Heart of Palestinian Suffering." Bethlehem: Kairos Palestine, 2009. http://www.kairospalestine.ps/.

Kane, Alex. "Jewish Establishment Pulls Our of Interfaith Dialogue . . . " *Mondoweiss.* October 2012. http://mondoweiss .net/2012/10/jewish-establishment-pulls-out-of-interfaith-dialogue-threatens-congressional-investigation-of-delegitimizers-over-christian-letter.html.

Kells, Brad E., Frank Ritchey Ames, and Jacob Life Wright. *Interpreting Exile: Displacement and Deportation in Biblical and Modern Contexts.* Atlanta: Society of Biblical Literature, 2011.

Khalidi, Walid. *All That Remains: The Palestinian Villages Occupied and Depopulated by Israel in 1948.* Washington, DC: Insitute of Palestine Studies, 2006.

Khoury, Rafiq. "The Conflict of Narratives: From Memory to Prophecy." In Raheb, *The Invention of History,* 259–68.

Khoury, Rajeh. *Editorials for the Time to Come.* Jerusalem: Al-Liza', 1996.

Kiracofe, Klifford Attick. *Dark Crusade: Christian Zionism and US Foreign Policy.* New York: Tauris, 2009.

Kwok, Pui-lan. *Discovering the Bible in the Non-Biblical World.* Maryknoll, NY: Orbis Books, 1995.

Lauterbach, Jacob Z. "The Pharisees and Their Teachings." In Neusner, *Origins of Judaism*, 57–129.

Loubser, J. A. *Critical Review of Racial Theology in South Africa: The Apartheid Bible*. New York: Edwin Mellen Press, 1991.

Magness, Jodi. *The Archeology of Qumran and the Dead Sea Scrolls*. Grand Rapids, MI: Eerdmans, 2002.

Man, Michael. *The Sources of Social Power*. Vol. 1, *A History of Power from the Beginning to AD 1760*. Vol. 2, *The Rise of Classes and Nation-State 1760–1914*. Vol. 3, *Global Empires and Revolution 1890–1945*. Cambridge: Cambridge University Press, 1986, 1993, 2012.

Masalha, Nur. *The Bible and Zionism: Invented Traditions, Archeology, and Post-Colonialism in Palestine-Israel*. London, Zed Books, 2007.

———. *Expulsion of the Palestinians: The Concept of "Transfer" in Zionist Political Thought, 1882–1948*. Washington, DC: Institute for Palestine Studies, 1992.

———. *Imperial Israel and the Palestinians the Politics of Expansion*. Sterling: Pluto Press, 2002.

———. *A Land Without a People: Israel, Transfer, and the Palestinians, 1949–96*. London: Faber, 1996.

———. *The Palestinians in Israel: Is Israel the State of All Its Citizens and "Absentees"?* Haifa: Galilee Center for Social Research, 1993.

———. *The Palestinian Nakba: Decolonizing History, Narrating the Subaltern, Reclaiming Memory*. London: Zed Books, 2012.

McNeil, Kristine. "The War of Academic Freedom." 25 November 2002. *The Nation*. http://www.thenation.com/article/war-academic-freedom.

Mearsheimer, John J., and Stephen M. Walt. *The Israel Lobby and US Foreign Policy*. New York: Farrar, Straus, and Giroux, 2007.

Mieroop, Marc Van De. *A History of the Ancient Near East ca. 3000–323 BC*. Malden, MA: Blackwell Publishing, 2007.

MIFTAH. "Palestinian Prisoners." June 2012. http://www.miftah.org/Doc/Factsheets/Miftah/English/Prisoners.pdf.

Mizrachi, Yonathan. "Between Holiness and Propaganda." Jerusalem: Emek Shaveh, December 2011. http:///www.alt-arch.org/oldcity.php.

Morris, Benny. *The Birth of the Palestinian Refugee Problem Revisited.* Cambridge: Cambridge University Press, 2004.

Moxnes, Halvor. *Jesus and the Rise of Nationalism: A New Quest for the Nineteenth-Century Historical Jesus.* New York: Tauris, 2012.

Moxnes, Halvor, Ward Blanton, and James G. Crossley, eds. *Jesus Beyond Nationalism: Constructing the Historical Jesus in a Period of Cultural Complexity.* London: Equinox, 2009.

Neusner, Jacob. *Origins of Judaism: The Pharisees and Other Sects (Vol. II, part 2).* New York: Garland, 1990.

O'Brien, Julia M. "The Hermeneutical Predicament: Why We Do Not Read the Bible in the Same Way and Why It Matters for Palestinian Advocacy." In Raheb, *The Biblical Text in the Context of Occupation*, 159–79.

Pappe, Ilan. *The Ethnic Cleansing of Palestine.* Oxford: Oneworld, 2006.

———. *Out of Frame: The Struggle for Academic Freedom in Israel.* New York: Pluto, 2010.

"Pillage of the Dead Sea: Israel's Unlawful Exploitation of Natural Resources in the Occupied Palestinian Territory." *Al-Haq.* September 3, 2012. http://www.alhaq.org/advocacy/topics/housing-land-and-natural-resources/621–israels-unlawful-exploitation-of-natural-resources-in-the-occupied-palestinian-territory.

Prior, Michael. *The Bible and Colonialism: A Moral Critique.* Sheffield: Sheffield Academic Press, 1997.

Raheb, Mitri. *Bethlehem Besieged.* Minneapolis: Augsburg-Fortress, 2004.

———. "Displacement Theopolitics." In Raheb, *The Invention of History*, 9–32.

———. *I Am a Palestinian Christian.* Minneapolis: Augsburg-Fortress, 1995.

———, ed. *The Biblical Text in the Context of Occupation: Towards a New Hermeneutics of Liberation.* Bethlehem: Diyar, 2012.

———. *God's Reign and People's Rule: Constitution, Religion, and Identity in Palestine.* Berlin: Aphorisma, 2009.

———. *The Invention of History: A Century of Interplay Between Theology and Politics in Palestine.* Bethlehem: Diyar, 2011.

Rantisi, Audeh. *Blessed are the Peacemakers: A Palestinian Christian in the West Bank.* Grand Rapids, MI: Zondervan, 1990.

Sabbah, Michel. *Pray for Peace in Jerusalem*. Jerusalem: Latin Patriarchate of Jerusalem, 1990.

————. *In Pulcritudini Pacis*. Jerusalem: Latin Patriarchate of Jerusalem, 1988.

————. *Preparation for the Jubilee for 2000*. Jerusalem: Latin Patriarchate of Jerusalem, 1997.

————. *Reading the Bible Today in the Land of the Bible*. Jerusalem: Latin Patriarchate of Jerusalem, 1993.

————. *Seek the Peace and Pursue It*. Jerusalem: Latin Patriarchate of Jerusalem 1998.

Said, Edward. *Orientalism*. New York: Random House, 1978.

Sand, Shlomo. *The Invention of the Jewish People*. London: Verso, 2009.

————. *The Invention of the Land of Israel: From Holy Land to Homeland*. London: Verso, 2012.

Scobbie, Iain, and Alon Margalit. "The Israeli Military Commander's Powers Under the Law of Occupation in Relation to Quarrying Activity in Area C." Diakonia. July 4, 2012. http://www.diakonia.se/documents/public/IHL/Berenice/Scobbie_Margalit_Expert_Opinion_Quarrying_West_Bank_September2012.pdf.

Segal, Rafi, and Eyal Weizmann, eds. *A Civilian Occupation: The Politics of Israeli Architecture*. London: Verso, 2003.

Sizer, Stephen. *Christian Zionism: Road Map to Armageddon?* Leicester: Inter-Varsity, 2004.

————. *Zion's Christian Soldiers? The Bible, Israel and the Church*. Nottingham: Inter-Varsity, 2007.

Smith, Robert. "American Expansionism, Theologies, and the Israel-Palestine Question." In Raheb, *The Invention of History*, 185–210.

————. "Interpreting the Bible, Interpreting the World: Anglo-American Christian Zionism and Palestinian Christian Concerns." In Raheb, *The Biblical Text in the Context of Occupation*, 147–58.

————. *More Desired Than Our Own Salvation: The Roots of Christian Zionism*. New York: Oxford University Press, 2013.

Sugirtharajah, R. S. *Exploring Postcolonial Biblical Criticism: History, Method, Practice*. Malden, MA: Blackwell, 2012.

————. *The Postcolonial Bible*, vol. 1 in the Bible and Post-Colonialism series. Sheffield: Sheffield Academic Press, 1998.

Tamari, Salim. *Mountain Against the Sea: Essays on Palestinian Society and Culture.* Berkeley and Los Angeles: University of California Press, 2009.

Tinker, George E. *Missionary Conquest: The Gospel and Native Americam Cultural Genocide.* Minneapolis: Augsburg-Fortress, 1993.

UNISPAL. "Farming Without Land, Fishing Without Water: Gaza Agricultural Sector Struggles to Survive." Unispal. May 2010. http://unispal.un.org/UNISPAL.NSF/0/9A265F2A909E9 A1D8525772E004FC34B.

United Nations. "General Assembly Votes Overwhelmingly to Accord Palestine 'Non-member Observer State' Status in United Nations." GA/11317. November 29, 2012. http://www .un.org/News/Press/docs/2012/ga11317.doc.htm.

United Nations Development Programme (UNDP). "The Arab Human Development Report 2005: Towards the Rise of Women in the Arab World." 2005. http://www.arab-hdr.org/ publications/other/ahdr/ahdr2005e.pdf.

United Nations Office for the Coordination of Humanitarian Affairs (UN OCHA). "Movement and Access in the West Bank." September 2011. http://unispal.un.org/UNISPAL.NSF/ 0/8F5CBCD2F464B6B18525791800541DA6.

United Nations Relief and Works Agency for Palestine Refugees in the Near East (UNRWA). "Palestine Refugees." October 20, 2012. http://www.unrwa.org/etemplate.php?id=86.

Wagner, Don. *Anxious for Armageddon: A Call to Partnership for Middle Eastern and Western Christians.* Scottdale, PA: Herald Press, 1995.

Warrior, Robert Allen. "A North American Perspective: Canaanites, Cowboys, and Indians." In *Voices from the Margin: Interpreting the Bible in the Third World*, edited by R. S. Sugirtharajah, 287–95. Maryknoll, NY: Orbis Books, 1991.

Whitelam, Keith. *The Invention of Ancient Israel: The Silencing of Palestinian History.* New York: Routledge, 1996.

Wright, Jacob L. "The Commemoration of Defeat and the Formation of a Nation in the Hebrew Bible." *Proof* 29 (2009): 433–72.

Yilmaz, Huseyin. "The Eastern Question and the Ottoman Empire: The Genesis of the Near and Middle East in the Nineteenth

Century." In Bonine, Amanat, and Gasper, *Is There a Middle East?* 11–35.

Younan, Munib. *Our Shared Witness: A Voice for Justice and Reconciliation.* Minneapolis: Lutheran University Press, 2012.

———. *Witnessing for Peace in Jerusalem and the World.* Edited by Fred Strickert. Minneapolis: Augsburg-Fortress, 2003.

Zaru, Jean. *Occupied with Nonviolence: A Palestinian Woman Speaks.* Minneapolis: Augsburg-Fortress, 2008.

Zeitoun, Mark. *Power and Water in the Middle East: The Hidden Politics of the Palestinian-Israeli Water Conflict.* London: Tauris, 2009.

Zertal, Idith, and Akiva Eldar. *Die Herren des landes: Israel und die Siedlerbewegung seit 1967.* Munich: DVA, 2007.

Websites of Interest:

Dar al-Kalima: http://www.daralkalima.edu.ps/

Diyar: http://www.diyar.ps/

Ecumenical Accompaniment Programme in Palestine and Israel: http://www.eappi.org

Evangelicals for Middle East Understanding: http://www.emeu.net/

Kairos Palestine: http://www.kairospalestine.ps

Mitri Rabeb: http://www.mitriraheb.org

Palestinian BDS National Committee: http://www.bdsmovement.net/

Project for the New American Century: http://www.newamericancentury.org/

Resource Center for Palestinian Residency and Refugee Rights: http://www.badil.org/en/historical-overview

Index